In case of loss, please return to:

_____

_____

_____

_____

As a reward: $ _____

D1648890

CREATION UNRAVELED

THE **GOSPEL** ACCORDING TO **GENESIS**

MATT CARTER
& HALIM SUH

Published by LifeWay Press®
© 2011 The Austin Stone Community Church

ISBN: 978-1-4158-7000-6
Item: 005378211

Dewey Decimal Classification Number: 222.11
Subject Heading: BIBLE. O.T. GENESIS—STUDY \ CREATION \ CHRISTIANITY

Printed in the United States of America.

Leadership and Adult Publishing
LifeWay Church Resources
One LifeWay Plaza
Nashville, Tennessee 37234-0175

We believe the Bible has God for its author; salvation for its end; and truth, without any mixture of error, for its matter and that all Scripture is totally true and trustworthy. The 2000 statement of *The Baptist Faith and Message* is our doctrinal guideline.

Cover design by Matt Lehman

TABLE OF CONTENTS

ICON LEGEND

 Things to listen to

 Things to watch

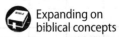 Expanding on biblical concepts

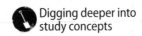 Fun facts and useful tidbits of information

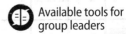 Digging deeper into study concepts

Available tools for group leaders

 On the Web

MATT CARTER

My name is Matt Carter. I serve as the lead pastor of The Austin Stone Community Church, which has grown from a core team of 15 people to more than 7,000 Sunday attendees since the church began in 2002. My desire to see the church become an advocate for the welfare of the city of Austin has led to the creation of a network that exists to actively pursue the redemption and renewal of the city for the advancement of the gospel. The For the City Network provides a platform for organizational collaboration by offering physical space to local nonprofits and creating a funnel for volunteer engagement. In addition to pastoring at The Austin Stone, I'm a cancer survivor, co-author of *For the City*, and speaker for camps and conferences nationwide. I hold a Master of Divinity from Southwestern Baptist Theological Seminary. I'm married to Jennifer, and we have three children: John Daniel, Annie, and Samuel.

HALIM SUH

Jesus Christ saved me. That's my story. God called me by His grace and won my rebellious heart forever. I am Halim Suh, and I serve as the pastor of equipping at The Austin Stone. I met my wife, Angela, at Texas A&M University. We met, dated, broke up (she with me), dated again (she came to her senses), and got married in 2002. Following college and marriage, I got a Master of Divinity from Southwestern Baptist Theological Seminary. After five years of marriage, we decided it was time to add some children to our family when we got the news that my mom's cancer had returned and would most likely be terminal. We prayed that God would grace us with a child before my mom went to be with Jesus. God answered our prayers, and Malachi was born three months before my mom passed away. Since then God has blessed us with two more children, our daughter Evangeline (Evie) and our son Moses (Mojo). We look forward to adding a couple more kiddos to our family through adoption.

GOD MADE IT GOOD AND WE BROKE IT BAD

BY MATT CARTER

GROWING UP, I WENT TO SUNDAY SCHOOL AND LEARNED ALL THE BIBLE STORIES. During my years at Texas A&M University, I sat under an amazing preacher who preached through the Bible verse by verse. I studied theology through seven grueling years of seminary. After starting The Austin Stone Community Church, I spent four and a half years preaching through the Book of John and two and a half years preaching through 1 Corinthians. But the truth of the matter is, nothing has given me a better understanding of the gospel of Jesus and the purpose of the cross than studying the Old Testament Book of Genesis. Genesis hasn't only increased my knowledge of the gospel; it's also increased my love for the gospel.

BELOW THE SURFACE

Because I grew up in the church, the stories of Genesis were some of the most familiar to me, like they may be to you. I have distinct memories of learning about Noah, the flood, the animals that came two by two, and the rainbow, which showed God's grace and promise that He wouldn't destroy the earth like that again. But only after preaching through Genesis did I realize how this story points us directly to the cross.

Or consider the story of Sodom and Gomorrah. If you asked the average church goer what that story is about, most would answer that it's about God's judgment against two cities for their sins. But what if the story of Sodom and Gomorrah is about more than that? What if it's one of the greatest illustrations of God's grace in all of Scripture, because the focus isn't on God's willingness to destroy sinners, but His willingness to *not* destroy sinners if one person among them is righteous?

> THE BIBLE ISN'T A COLLECTION OF STORIES, EACH WITH ITS OWN MORAL PRINCIPLES AND RULES TO ADD TO THE LONG LIST OF THINGS WE MUST DO TO PLEASE GOD. RATHER, THE BIBLE TELLS US ONE GRAND STORY.

I saw this pattern repeated over and over again throughout the stories in Genesis and the rest of the Old Testament. That's when I truly understood that the Bible isn't a collection of stories, each with its own moral principles and rules to add to the long list of things we must do to please God. Rather, the Bible tells us One Grand Story—the story of the one and only God who created humanity, humanity's rebellion against Him, and the ruins that were left in the wake of our rebellion. This is *creation unraveled*.

But the story continues, and Genesis through Revelation tell about God moving heaven and earth to re-create His world and make all things new—*creation restored*. The story of the Bible isn't primarily about all the things *we* must do to be good and moral people. It's the story of everything *God* has done to bring us back to Himself. Through the Book of Genesis, we see that Christ didn't come to earth to make bad people better; He came to make dead people alive. Genesis provides one of the clearest illustrations of the gospel in the Bible.

THE FOUNDATION OF THE GOSPEL

Perhaps you've never sought to dig deeply into the Genesis accounts of creation, the flood, or Abraham, Isaac, and Jacob because, like me, you've heard them taught so many times that you feel like you know them inside and out. Or maybe you avoid them because you feel uncomfortable with some of God's characteristics in the Old Testament.

THROUGH THE BOOK OF GENESIS, WE SEE THAT CHRIST DIDN'T COME TO EARTH TO MAKE A BAD PEOPLE BETTER; HE CAME TO MAKE A DEAD PEOPLE ALIVE.

Regardless of our presuppositions, it's critical to realize that though the New Testament reveals the fulfillment of the gospel in Jesus, the Old Testament reveals the foundation for that very same gospel.

The words we read in Genesis are the same words that provided hope for hungry Israelites in the wilderness, breathed courage into the heart of David in the most difficult moments of his life, and fed the soul of Jesus Himself during His time on earth. There's no other God besides the God of Genesis. We encourage you to open the Book of Genesis with us and encounter our great and living God. In Him you'll find an immovable anchor that keeps you in Christ Jesus all the days of your life.

FOR FURTHER STUDY

In this book, we walk you through a high-level, big picture study of Genesis 1–11, but the Book of Genesis doesn't stop there. That's why we've also written *Creation Restored*, a look at the foreshadowing of the gospel in the lives of Abraham, Jacob, and Joseph as told in Genesis 12–50. Visit *threadsmedia.com/creationrestored* to find out more about *Creation Restored* and continue your study of the gospel according to Genesis.

IN THE BEGINNING WAS JESUS

GENESIS 1

SESSION ONE

"In the beginning God created the heavens and the earth. Now the earth was formless and empty, darkness covered the surface of the watery depths, and the Spirit of God was hovering over the surface of the waters. Then God said, 'Let there be light,' and there was light" (Genesis 1:1-3).

When we hear the word gospel, we think about the first four books of the New Testament. When we hear the word gospel, we think about Jesus and the cross. When we hear the word gospel, we think about miracles, grace, and salvation. When we hear the word gospel, we don't think about the Book of Genesis. At least I (Matt) never did.

Most people associate a study of Genesis with creation, evolution, intelligent design, the patriarchs, the usual. But did you know that the gospel can be seen just as clearly in Genesis 1 as Luke 19? Would it surprise you to hear that the cross is spoken of as early as Genesis 3? The truth is, you can't get three verses into the first chapter of the first book of the Bible before you see evidence of the gospel.

The gospel refers to God's redemption and restoration of a rebellious people back to Himself for His glory and our good. It's about God taking a creation that has unraveled as a consequence of the sin of man and restoring it back to its original purpose and design. This is the message of the One Grand Story of Scripture, and it's the genesis of the Book of Genesis—the beginning of the beginning.

BEFORE WE BEGIN

To begin a study of the Book of Genesis (or any book of the Bible for that matter), one of the most important things to keep in mind is the author's intended purpose for the book. Good hermeneutics, that is, good interpretation and study of God's Word, starts by taking into consideration the original author, audience, and historical context. Our natural reaction is to bring our expectations, thoughts, feelings, and culture to a text, so this can be a challenging starting point for us.

We tend to view Scripture through the lens of our circumstances. Sometimes that's the only way we know how to approach the Bible. However, this approach is dangerous. When we open up the Word of God, the first thing we should do is lay our presuppositions aside in order to seek the true meaning of the text. Then we can apply that meaning to our lives. We can't shortcut this process. The Holy Spirit will work, not in spite of a biblical author's intended purpose, but through that purpose.

Most theologians and biblical scholars agree that the author of Genesis is Moses, and no one questions that the original intended audience was *not* a 21st-century one. When we encounter passages like Genesis 1:1, we have in the back of our minds cultural influences such as the creation debates about when and how the universe came into existence. While contemplating the details of creation can be important and interesting, we must remember that Moses didn't write Genesis' opening words

Listen to "Beautiful Things" by Gungor from the *Creation Unraveled* playlist, available at *threadsmedia.com/creationunraveled.*

SESSION ONE CREATION UNRAVELED

with our modern scientific debates in mind. He also didn't write to silence critics who question the existence of God.

Moses' original audience was a B.C. Jewish one—the Israelites of the ancient Near East. They didn't have a scientific paradigm to ask the questions raised by later generations, and they weren't questioning God's existence or how the world came to be. Moses' intent in the first verses of Genesis was to show the pattern for how God was going to deal with not only the formless and void world, but the formless and void hearts of the men and women who rejected Him.

Genesis chapters 1 and 2 raise many disputed issues, from Young Earth to Old Earth creationism, to theistic or non-theistic evolution and the acceptance or rejection of intelligent design altogether. For those of you interested, a whole slew of books exist that address the many debates surrounding creation.[1] But for the purpose of this study, we're going to focus on the dominant theological emphasis in the text—the evidence of the gospel. So we'll begin by asking ourselves, *What is the context of this passage?* But before we answer this question, consider the following illustration on the importance of context:

I have three children. My third child has affectionately earned the nickname "Hurricane Sammy." Imagine you're my neighbor, and you see me running around my front lawn chasing after Sammy. My face is bright red, and the veins in my neck are bulging as I'm yelling at him. It's apparent that I've completely lost my cool, and you don't know what I'm going to do once I get my hands on him. If that's the only thing you see, you may wonder if I'm an abusive father. You may even keep a close eye on me for fear that you need to turn me in to the police. And all of that is because you don't know my intention.

Instead of keeping all of these suspicions to yourself, what if you talked to me to find out what was really going on? Then you'd find out that I was angry at Sammy because he was running around with a stick trying to hit his sister on the head. Doesn't that change everything? Doesn't finding out my intent and purpose for acting the way I did clarify the situation?

IDOL-WORSHIPING ISRAELITES

The Israelites, Moses' original audience for Genesis, were en route to the promised land. If they weren't asking questions about intelligent design and how long the earth had been around, what questions were they asking? What were the issues in their lives and hearts that would've impacted Moses' writing?

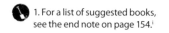 1. For a list of suggested books, see the end note on page 154.[1]

We learn from various passages in the Bible that the Israelites had a problem with building and worshiping idols. They were quick to worship gods they believed had the power to save and rescue them, despite their relationship with the one true God. They had a deep and constant inclination of their hearts toward evil, and idolatry is a natural overflow of this sinful state.[2] All the writers of the Old Testament, Moses included, repeatedly had to remind the people of God that the God of Israel is *the Lord*, and their idols could never match His power. God alone is uncreated. He created the heavens and the earth and every molecule and atom they (and we) encounter.

> **"For the LORD is great and is highly praised; He is feared above all gods. For all the gods of the peoples are idols, but the LORD made the heavens"** (Psalm 96:4-5).

The root of Israel's problem was a lack of belief and trust in the power and might of God. Throughout the Old Testament, including Psalm 96, writers knitted together stories, poems, and exhortations to remind the Israelites that their God is powerful and mighty; that He alone is able to save.

Moses' introductory sentences in the Book of Genesis reveal to the Israelites the power and might of their God. His intent was to help his Jewish audience understand that the God of their bedtime stories, the God of their fathers, the God of Abraham, Isaac, and Jacob, and the God of Moses was the very same God who created the world. Moses said to his audience, "He is *your* God, the God of Israel, who was the catalyst for, and the Author and Creator of, everything."

So, if Genesis was written for idol-worshiping Israelites, how does it intersect with our lives? Answering that question is the purpose behind this study. Because of our unique position in history, we're able to hold the completed Bible in our hands. When we read Genesis, we do so in light of all of Scripture, including the New Testament. Genesis doesn't mean less to us than it did to the Israelites; it means more.

Moses' original intent for writing Genesis still remains applicable for us. The pages of this book reveal who our God is and remind us that above all else, He's our God. But with the completed Scripture in our hands and the Holy Spirit bringing it to life, we see that not only is our God a God who speaks into a formless and void world to create light, but He also speaks into formless and void hearts to create "the light of the knowledge of God's glory in the face of Jesus" (2 Corinthians 4:6).

FORMLESS AND VOID

From the very beginning, thousands of years before the name of Jesus was uttered, we

---

 2. The apostle Paul gave a powerful condemnation of idolatry and the sins it leads to in Romans 1:21-32.

SESSION ONE CREATION UNRAVELED

see echoes of the gospel. In Genesis 1:3 we get a glimpse of the One who would come to this earth and shine His light into the darkness of our hearts. Listen to how the earth is described in Genesis 1:

> **"In the beginning God created the heavens and the earth. The earth was formless and void, and darkness was over the surface of the deep, and the Spirit of God was moving over the surface of the waters" (Genesis 1:1-2, ESV).**

In the beginning the earth was formless. God had not yet "established the earth," or "fixed its dimensions," or "stretched a measuring line across it" (Job 38:4-5). There was no order; chaos reigned. In the beginning the earth was void. It was empty. God had not yet filled the land with vegetation and livestock, the ocean with fish, or the heavens with stars.

The Hebrew wording for "formless and void" (*tohu* and *bohu*) is very specific, conveying the idea of utter chaos and complete disorder.[3] On top of that chaos, we read that it was dark. So, God created the heavens and the earth, but the earth was chaotic, dark, cold, and uninhabitable. The world was lifeless.

ECHOES OF THE GOSPEL

That remained the state of the earth until God spoke into the darkness and chaos:

> **"Then God said, 'Let there be light,' and there was light" (Genesis 1:3).**

God spoke! And when He spoke, light appeared. And from this light came life. Life started springing up in every shape, form, and color. God looked at what was once dark, cold, and chaotic and said, "Now that is *good!*"

Do you hear the echo of the gospel in God's command for light in the midst of darkness? Do you see God setting the stage for a greater plan through those simple words in the very beginning? The Israelites continually struggled to worship the Creator instead of their creations. Why? Because their hearts were filled with darkness and void of goodness:

> **"When the Lord saw that man's wickedness was widespread on the earth and that every scheme his mind thought of was nothing but evil all the time . . . " (Genesis 6:5).**

And in truth, humanity hasn't changed in that regard. We may live thousands of years later, but Paul's description of human life apart from God still fits:

---

 3. Or "confusion and emptiness," as the words are rendered in Isaiah 34:11 (ESV).

 In verse 2, the reference to "the Spirit of God moved" literally means "continued brooding over it," as a fowl does when hatching eggs.[ii]

"They are darkened in their understanding, excluded from the life of God, because of the ignorance that is in them and because of the hardness of their hearts" (Ephesians 4:18).

Just as in the beginning God commanded light to shine in the midst of utter darkness, He has shone the light of His Son Jesus into our darkened hearts:

"For God who said, 'Let light shine out of darkness,' has shone in our hearts to give the light of the knowledge of God's glory in the face of Jesus Christ" (2 Corinthians 4:6).

In addition to light in the darkness, the second echo of the gospel we see in creation is that God speaks form into the formless and creates order from chaos. In the first three days of creation, God addressed the formlessness of the earth:

"Then God said, 'Let there be light,' and there was light. God saw that the light was good, and God separated the light from the darkness. God called the light 'day,' and He called the darkness 'night.' Evening came and then morning: the first day.

"Then God said, 'Let there be an expanse between the waters, separating water from water.' So God made the expanse and separated the water under the expanse from the water above the expanse. And it was so. God called the expanse 'sky.' Evening came and then morning: the second day.

"Then God said, 'Let the water under the sky be gathered into one place, and let the dry land appear.' And it was so. God called the dry land 'earth,' and He called the gathering of the water 'seas.' And God saw that it was good" (Genesis 1:3-10).

To bring order to the chaos of the world, God created time periods of day and night. He also gave the unruly waters boundaries and said, "Only this far will you come and no further," so that order exists between the water and heaven and the water and dry land. Again we see in creation the foreshadowing of the gospel in our lives. Read how the apostle Paul described the chaos that results from his wrestling with sin:

"For I do not understand what I am doing, because I do not practice what I want to do, but I do what I hate. And if I do what I do not want to do, I agree with the law that it is good. So now I am no longer the one doing it, but it is sin living in me. For I know that nothing good lives in me, that is, in my

Watch the *Creation Unraveled* video "In the Beginning Was Jesus," available at *threadsmedia.com/creationunraveled*.

flesh. For the desire to do what is good is with me, but there is no ability to do it. For I do not do the good that I want to do, but I practice the evil that I do not want to do. Now if I do what I do not want, I am no longer the one doing it, but it is the sin that lives in me. So I discover this principle: When I want to do what is good, evil is with me. For in my inner self I joyfully agree with God's law. But I see a different law in the parts of my body, waging war against the law of my mind and taking me prisoner to the law of sin in the parts of my body. What a wretched man I am! Who will rescue me from this dying body?" (Romans 7:15-24).

One word describes the state of Paul's heart—chaotic. He knew what was right, but he couldn't do it, and he knew what he was doing was wrong, but he couldn't stop. From within his struggles and the turmoil of his soul, Paul asked one question. His was the same question every person wrestling with sin has cried for generations: "Who will rescue me from this dying body?" Thankfully, Paul gave us an answer:

"I thank God through Jesus Christ our Lord! So then, with my mind I myself am a slave to the law of God, but with my flesh, to the law of sin. Therefore, no condemnation now exists for those in Christ Jesus . . . " (Romans 7:25–8:1).

Jesus is the answer to the chaotic struggle with sin in the human heart. The Word of God made flesh. It's true now, and it was true in the beginning. Only one thing can bring form and order in the midst of chaos—the Word of the Living God.

I challenge you to find one Christian whose story doesn't look like Paul's. No matter what country, culture, or century believers are from, if you ask them to describe their conversion experiences, they will speak stories of a God who brought joy into their sorrows, peace into their calamity, and order into their chaos.

The third echo of the gospel evident in the creation account is the way God dealt with what Scripture calls the "void." After remedying the darkness and the formlessness of the world, God addressed its emptiness. According to verses 11-25, He filled the earth with three different things—fruit, light, and life. These are the same things God uses to fill the void in our lives when we come to Him in faith and trust Christ's completed work on the cross for our salvation. Let's compare the Genesis verses with a few passages from the New Testament.

FRUIT
"Then God said, 'Let the earth produce vegetation: seed-bearing plants and fruit trees on the earth bearing fruit with seed in it according to their

 In a 2007 Barna Group survey, 60 percent of the adult population questioned said they take Genesis literally when it says God created the universe in six days.[iii]

kinds.' And it was so. The earth produced vegetation: seed-bearing plants according to their kinds and trees bearing fruit with seed in it according to their kinds. And God saw that it was good. Evening came and then morning: the third day" (Genesis 1:11-13).

"Remain in Me, and I in you. Just as a branch is unable to produce fruit by itself unless it remains on the vine, so neither can you unless you remain in Me. I am the vine; you are the branches. The one who remains in Me and I in him produces much fruit, because you can do nothing without Me" (John 15:4-5).

LIGHT

"Then God said, 'Let there be lights in the expanse of the sky to separate the day from the night. They will serve as signs for festivals and for days and years. They will be lights in the expanse of the sky to provide light on the earth.' And it was so. God made the two great lights—the greater light to have dominion over the day and the lesser light to have dominion over the night—as well as the stars. God placed them in the expanse of the sky to provide light on the earth, to dominate the day and the night, and to separate light from darkness. And God saw that it was good. Evening came and then morning: the fourth day" (Genesis 1:14-19). .

"You are the light of the world" (Matthew 5:14).

LIFE

"Then God said, 'Let the water swarm with living creatures, and let birds fly above the earth across the expanse of the sky.' So God created the large sea-creatures and every living creature that moves and swarms in the water, according to their kinds. He also created every winged bird according to its kind. And God saw that it was good. So God blessed them, 'Be fruitful, multiply, and fill the waters of the seas, and let the birds multiply on the earth. Evening came and then morning: the fifth day. Then God said, 'Let the earth produce living creatures according to their kinds: livestock, creatures that crawl, and the wildlife of the earth according to their kinds.' And it was so. So God made the wildlife of the earth according to their kinds, the livestock according to their kinds, and creatures that crawl on the ground according to their kinds. And God saw that it was good" (Genesis 1:20-25).

 Listen to "Our Great God" by Todd Agnew from the *Creation Unraveled* playlist, available at *threadsmedia. com/creationunraveled.*

"A thief comes only to steal and to kill and to destroy. I have come so that they may have life and have it in abundance" (John 10:10).

Before God produces fruit, light, and life in us, our hearts are void and empty. Our lives are devoid of anything good, joyful, or fulfilling, even if we've fooled ourselves into believing they aren't.

The life of one of our greatest church fathers, St. Augustine of Hippo, is a great example of this point. He left this world as one of the godliest men of faith who ever lived, but that wasn't always the case. His life was filled with emptiness and void, and he was plagued by sexual sins. But a day came when everything changed. Listen to the cry of his heart as he describes how God filled the void in his life:

"How sweet all at once it was for me to be rid of those fruitless joys which I had once feared to lose! . . . You drove them from me, you who are the true, the sovereign joy. You drove them from me and took their place, you who are sweeter than all pleasure."[4]

THE CREATION OF HUMANITY

Up to this point in Genesis, God had repeatedly foreshadowed the gospel in His creation of the universe, the plants, and the animals. Starting in verse 26, He shifted gears and focused on the creation of those who would be the recipients of the gospel.

"Then God said, 'Let Us make man in Our image, according to Our likeness. They will rule the fish of the sea, the birds of the sky, the livestock, all the earth, and the creatures that crawl on the earth.' So God created man in His own image; He created him in the image of God; He created them male and female" (Genesis 1:26-27).

Prior to these verses, God had created in a third person kind of way. He spoke a command to "let there be," and the universe obeyed. But God created differently when it came to humanity. Instead of saying "let there be," He said "let Us make." His creation of humanity was also distinct from the creation of the animals. While God created each of them "according to their kind," He created man and woman according to His very likeness. Special emphasis was given to the creation of humanity, the future recipients of the gospel:

"God blessed them, and God said to them, 'Be fruitful, multiply, fill the earth, and subdue it. Rule the fish of the sea, the birds of the sky, and every creature that crawls on the earth.' God also said, 'Look, I have given

4. As quoted in John Piper's *The Legacy of Sovereign Joy: God's Triumphant Grace in the Lives of Augustine, Luther, and Calvin* (Wheaton, Illinois: Crossway Books, 2000), 57.

you every seed-bearing plant on the surface of the entire earth and every tree whose fruit contains seed. This food will be for you, for all the wildlife of the earth, for every bird of the sky, and for every creature that crawls on the earth—everything having the breath of life in it. I have given every green plant for food.' And it was so. God saw all that He had made, and it was very good. Evening came and then morning: the sixth day" (Genesis 1:28-31).

In verses 28-31, Moses used poetic language to describe what God said to the first man and woman. The English translation of this passage makes the poetry difficult to see, but hints of it seep through. Notice the repetition of the word "every." This repetition mimics the stanzas of a poem or song. Imagine God singing a song over His most prized creation, and the only created being that He saw fit to wear His image—us.

When my (Halim) first child, Malachi, was born, I stood in that hospital room and held him in my arms. And even though up to this point all he had done was cost me a lot of money and caused my wife a lot of pain, as I held him in my arms for the very first time, I was crazy about him. I always wondered what my first interaction with my first child would be like and what my first words to him would be. In that moment I could only think of one thing to say to him: "Everything I have is yours."

Holding His most prized creation, His own children, in His arms, God sang over us and told us that everything He created was created for our benefit, and it was good. The word *good* shows up several times in the creation account. Out of God's own goodness, He created good things, and when He was finished, He reflected on His work:

> "God saw all that He had made, and it was very good" (Genesis 1:31).

In the midst of a dark, formless, and void world, God created light, order, and life. But what happened next in the history of this newly created world is what created the need for the gospel that we've been talking about: humanity's rejection of the goodness of God and the subsequent unraveling of all the "good" found in creation.

According to the New Testament passages we examined in this session, the gospel produces fruit, light, and life in the lives of its recipients. With this in mind, reflect on the following questions:

Where do you see *spiritual fruit* in your life?

When I approach life with the Joy Peace & Patience.

Where do you see *spiritual light* in your life?

The lord reveals area's I need to Change.

Where do you see *spiritual life* in your life?

When I act out my faith, with my Kids & those around me.

God creates order where there's chaos. What would your life be like if God hadn't saved you? What do you think you'd be doing, and how do you think you'd be living?

I cant imagine my life without God! I would probably be in a terrible - abusive relationship with a disease - mindlessly living very selfishly.

Leading a group? It's the way to go. Find extra questions and teaching tools in the leader kit, available at *threadsmedia.com/creationunraveled.*

Consider the echoes of the gospel in the creation account as you think about the following questions:

Is it hard to believe your heart was dark and empty apart from Christ? Why or why not?

No because I "feel" empty when I am not walking with him. I feel Alone & lonliness is a Dark Place!

Think of non-Christians in your life. In what ways do you expect them to behave as if they have life in their hearts? In what ways have you put the pressure on yourself or on them to come to know God instead of acknowledging that He alone is capable of making life?

Somehow believe that "I" can change their "Darkness" I get frustrated when they dont see His Awesome Power & Goodness!

God's work alone makes dead hearts alive. Is that frustrating to you or relieving? How does it make you feel and why?

Frustrating Until I finally Realized how True it is & then Such a Relief to just finally turn people over to him!

Other than God, what do you "worship"? Do you look to relationships to make you feel safe and secure? Do your possessions give you worth? Do your skills/abilities or the roles you're in provide you with security, approval, or power?

Definetly see how my Athletic abilities made me feel capable & Good about myself & I enjoyed the Praise & admiration I recieved. — I use to look to "Boys" or my husband for security & NOW I know the Lord is All I need to make me Worthy! — I worship myself & my needs @ times.

Compare the things or people you listed in the previous question with the God of creation. How might His power over creation lead you to worship and trust in Him instead of idols?

Praise God! He is helping me to Not be so focused on myself & "my wants" & desires.
      Lord I pray You continue the work you have begun in me!

What are the dark places in your heart? How does God's power to create something from nothing give you hope of change in those areas?

If the Lord can Create the magnificent Universe — He can most certainly — Begin & Complete A change In Me!

Carry it to Completion!

THE BIGNESS AND NEARNESS OF GOD

GENESIS 1 & 2

SESSION TWO

"Then the LORD God formed the man out of the dust from the ground and breathed the breath of life into his nostrils, and the man became a living being. The LORD God planted a garden in Eden, in the east, and there He placed the man He had formed" (Genesis 2:7-8).

On my (Matt) way to church to preach the sermon on "The Bigness and Nearness of God," I was listening to Chris Tomlin's Christmas CD Glory in the Highest. If you've listened to this CD, you know it's an excellent album (so good that it wasn't Christmastime but I was listening to it anyway). I've always loved Christmas music and wish we could sing Christmas songs year-round. With my sermon occupying my thoughts, I had an epiphany: Most Christmas songs have a variation of the same two themes. First, the power and transcendence of God. To say God is transcendent speaks to His being above or beyond us. It communicates His "bigness" and power. But the focus of Christmas is on the incarnation, God coming to be with us, and that touches on the other theme—God's nearness. These two themes aren't present only in Christmas songs, though. They permeate all of Scripture, and we see the juxtaposition of God's bigness with His nearness first in Genesis chapters 1 and 2.

GOD'S COMPLEX CHARACTER

Because God's bigness and nearness can be misunderstood as conflicting traits, it's not unusual to find ourselves thinking about Him as if He has multiple personalities. We see Him acting one way in the Old Testament—like a judge concerned with justice, power, and majesty—and a different way in the New Testament—tender and humble as a lamb.

Contemporary Christians have been known to make the mistake of thinking that God had a personality makeover. People didn't like Him in the Old Testament, so He decided to be nicer in the New Testament. You may have heard someone refer to "the God of the Old Testament" versus "the God of the New Testament," alluding to a change in His personality during the 400-year gap between the Testaments. However, the Book of Hebrews takes that thought off the table:

"Jesus Christ is the same yesterday, today, and forever" (Hebrews 13:8).

God's character is so much more complex than ours that it's difficult for us to wrap our minds around the aspects of His personality. Sometimes He seems tender and sweet, but then at other times He's stern and wrathful. You may never have said it out loud, but have you ever wondered, *Is God bipolar? Which God will I get when I approach Him today? The angry, just, and transcendent One or the kind and loving Friend who's "closer than a brother"?* The problem is that instead of dealing with the seeming contradictions in God's character, it's easier for us to default to creating God in our image.

Listen to "Beautiful Mystery" by Aaron Ivey from the *Creation Unraveled* playlist, available at *threadsmedia. com/creationunraveled*.

SESSION TWO CREATION UNRAVELED

We prefer a god who is only about justice and wrath, a scary god for sure, but at least a predictable one. Or a god who is only forgiving and loving. He may not seem powerful or majestic, but at least He's kind. Instead of appreciating the complexities in God's character and seeing Him for who He truly is—transcendent *and* intimate, big *and* near—we package Him into a god we can manage and understand. Without meaning to, we end up worshiping a god of our own creation.

However, if we're to know God as He truly is, we must understand that He isn't kind and loving sometimes, while sovereign and just at others. He's always both. He's powerful and sovereign in His loving-kindness, and He's kind and loving in His power and sovereignty. God is both lovingly fierce and fiercely loving. This is the unfathomable picture of God Moses painted for us in Genesis 1 and 2.

ELOHIM AND YAHWEH

The Book of Genesis opens with a prologue, in which Moses unpacks for us the creation of the heavens and the earth. Moses described the power and majesty of God, which was on display as all of creation was formed by His words and hands. At the start of chapter 2, Moses transitioned to giving "accounts," or retellings of events. The first account begins in Genesis 2:4, when Moses retold the account of creation. Anyone else having a sense of déjà vu?

It may seem as though we've hit rewind and are listening to the same story again, but if we take a closer look at a comparison of the two chapters, a particular distinction becomes evident. Moses is retelling the story of creation but with a slightly different twist. The result is an illustration of the bigness and nearness of God.

Let's look again at chapter 1 and observe how Moses referred to God:

> "Then *God* said, 'Let the earth produce living creatures according to their kinds: livestock, creatures that crawl, and the wildlife of the earth according to their kinds.' And it was so. So *God* made the wildlife of the earth according to their kinds, the livestock according to their kinds, and creatures that crawl on the ground according to their kinds. And *God* saw that it was good. Then *God* said, 'Let Us make man in Our image, according to Our likeness. They will rule the fish of the sea, the birds of the sky, the livestock, all the earth, and the creatures that crawl on the earth.' So *God* created man in His own image; He created him in the image of *God*; He created them male and female" (Genesis 1:24-27, emphasis added).

In Genesis 1, the Hebrew word used for God is *Elohim*. But from the looks of our English translation, Moses simply referred to God as *God*. We'll see the significance of that shortly. But first, let's compare the Genesis 1 passage with a few verses from Genesis 2:

> "These are the records of the heavens and the earth, concerning their creation at the time that the LORD God made the earth and the heavens. No shrub of the field had yet grown on the land, and no plant of the field had yet sprouted, for the LORD God had not made it rain on the land, and there was no man to work the ground. But water would come out of the ground and water the entire surface of the land. Then the LORD God formed the man out of the dust from the ground and breathed the breath of life into his nostrils, and the man became a living being. The LORD God planted a garden in Eden, in the east, and there He placed the man He had formed" (Genesis 2:4-8, emphasis added).

Although chapter 2 starts out like a repeat of the prologue, the two chapters have one noticeable distinction—the name Moses used for God. In verses 4-8 of chapter 2 and following, Moses referred to God as "the LORD God," the translation of the Hebrew word *Yahweh*. The two different names Moses used for God reveal something about who He is. The question is, what?

Elohim is a generic name for "God" that means "might, power, majesty, or all-mightiness." It represents God's transcendence, His otherness, and His bigness. Chapter 1 speaks of the great Elohim who created the heavens with a single word. Elohim said, "Let there be light," and bam! There was light. When Elohim spoke, everything obeyed. Light came into existence, waters parted, and the universe was born.

But as chapter 2 begins, Moses suddenly shifts to calling God *Yahweh*. Yahweh isn't one of the names for God that describes His role or an attribute of His character. Yahweh is God's personal name; it's the name He calls Himself:[1]

> "God replied to Moses, 'I AM WHO I AM. This is what you are to say to the Israelites: I AM has sent me to you.' God also said to Moses, 'Say this to the Israelites: Yahweh, the God of your fathers, the God of Abraham, the God of Isaac, and the God of Jacob, has sent me to you. This is My name forever; this is how I am to be remembered in every generation'" (Exodus 3:14-15).

To help us understand the distinction, let's use me as an example. If you saw me walking down the hall and you had a friend with you, you might say to your friend, "Hey, that's

---

 1. God's personal name was so holy to the Israelites that it was blasphemous to speak the name; it was only written.

our pastor." In this case, pastor is my generic name, one that speaks to my role in your life. But if you stopped and introduced your friend to me, you would say, "Hey, this is my pastor, Matt," because Matt is my personal name.

Yahweh is the personal name of God, and as Moses emphasized that name over and over again in Genesis 2, his intent becomes evident. Yes, God is powerful, transcendent, and big, but that very same God is also personal. He is intimate and near. He is someone who can be known.

While chapter 1 paints the picture of the almighty Elohim creating all things with His word, chapter 2 shows us Yahweh bending down to form man out of the dust with His own hands and breathe life into him with His own breath.

GOD'S BIGNESS AND NEARNESS IN SCRIPTURE

Reflecting on God's bigness reminds me of the Old Testament story about King David's decision to bring the ark of the covenant back to Israel.[2] The ark of the covenant represented God's presence among the Israelites, and He gave them very specific instructions about how He wanted the ark transported when necessary. Only God's priests, the Levites, were allowed to carry the ark, and they were required to carry it on poles to avoid direct contact with it. These strict rules illustrate God's separateness and holiness. They show that He is Elohim.

But David, in his zeal to get the presence of God back to Jerusalem, ignored God's commands and sent some of his servants with an ox cart to pick up the ark. After they got it, they headed back for Jerusalem and were cruising along with the ark on the cart. Everyone was fired up and excited, until the cart hit a bump, and the ark of the covenant started teetering like it was going to topple off the cart. Then some poor guy named Uzzah reached up and touched it to keep it from falling over (which, for the record, is what I would do too if the box holding the presence of God was about to fall off a cart). And what does the Bible tell us happened? God "smote" him, to borrow a term from the King James Version (2 Samuel 6:7). Uzzah died right there on the spot.

Needless to say, when it came time to move the ark further, the Levites paid much closer attention to the commands God had given them. They placed the poles in the proper rings, picked up the ark, and placed the poles on their shoulders. Second Samuel 6:13 tells us they took six steps with the ark then set it back down and worshiped because God hadn't killed them. David and the Israelites with him learned something that day. Our God is the mighty Elohim, and He demands complete obedience.

2. Read the full account of this story in 2 Samuel 6.

Thousands of years later, the same God, on earth as Jesus the Son, was walking down the street in the midst of a crowd of people when a woman desperate to be healed from disease reached out and touched Him without His permission.[3] But unlike Uzzah, this woman experienced the opposite effect of touching the presence of God:

> **"Instantly her flow of blood ceased, and she sensed in her body that she was cured of her affliction" (Mark 5:29).**

Scripture says that Jesus felt His power go out of Him, but instead of punishing her for touching His cloak without invitation, Jesus commended the woman's faith (v. 34).

On the one hand, God killed someone for touching Him, because He is Elohim and must be obeyed. But on the other hand, the same God healed someone for touching Him, because He is Yahweh and is intimately involved in the lives of His children.

Consider another comparison. The Old Testament prophet Habakkuk began his oracle to the nation of Judah by crying out for God to intervene in the disobedience and apathy that he witnessed there. The Judeans tried to worship the one true God along with all the other gods around them. They were "kind of, sort of" being obedient to God. But God demands complete devotion from His people. Partial obedience is the same as complete disobedience in His eyes. And so His response to Habakkuk's plea for justice was to send the violent Chaldeans to punish them. Here is how God described the Chaldeans:

> **"Look at the nations and observe—be utterly astounded! For something is taking place in your days that you will not believe when you hear about it. Look! I am raising up the Chaldeans, that bitter, impetuous nation that marches across the earth's open spaces to seize territories not its own. They are fierce and terrifying; their views of justice and sovereignty stem from themselves. Their horses are swifter than leopards and more fierce than wolves of the night. Their horsemen charge ahead; their horsemen come from distant lands. They fly like an eagle, swooping to devour. All of them come to do violence; their faces are set in determination. They gather prisoners like sand. They mock kings, and rulers are a joke to them. They laugh at every fortress and build siege ramps to capture it" (Habakkuk 1:5-10).**

The Chaldeans were an absolutely ruthless people, and God sent them to destroy His own people—men, women, and children—because He is Elohim, and He is mighty and just. The Judeans learned that truth the hard way.

 "Yahweh, our Lord, how magnificent is Your name throughout the earth!" (Psalm 8:1).

 3. You can find the story of the woman Jesus healed in Mark 5:24-34.

SESSION TWO CREATION UNRAVELED

Fast-forward several centuries, and this same God in the flesh was standing in the temple court one day when a group of Pharisees dragged in a woman who had been caught in the act of adultery and threw her at His feet. The Pharisees pointed out to Jesus that according to the law, adulteresses were punished by stoning. This woman wasn't "kind of, sort of" sinning, like the Judeans Habakkuk spoke out against. She was caught in the act. How would you expect Jesus to respond to a woman caught breaking one of His Ten Commandments? Based on Habakkuk 1, you wouldn't expect this show of compassion:

> "Jesus stooped down and started writing on the ground with His finger. When they persisted in questioning Him, He stood up and said to them, 'The one without sin among you should be the first to throw a stone at her.' Then He stooped down again and continued writing on the ground. When they heard this, they left one by one, starting with the older men. Only He was left, with the woman in the center. When Jesus stood up, He said to her, 'Woman, where are they? Has no one condemned you?' 'No one, Lord,' she answered. 'Neither do I condemn you,' said Jesus. 'Go, and from now on do not sin anymore'" (John 8:6-11).

Jesus looked at the circle of Pharisees surrounding the poor woman and said, "Here's what we're going to do, boys. Whichever one of you in the circle has never sinned, you go ahead and throw the first rock." And after the Pharisees did a little math, they left. Was anyone in that circle sinless? Yes, but not one of the Pharisees. Only Jesus, God Himself, was without sin. Was Jesus qualified to throw the first stone at her? Absolutely. But He didn't do it. He looked down at the woman who was humiliated in her sin, helped her up, and sent her on her way, commanding her not to sin again.

On the one hand, God looked at the apathy of His people and destroyed them. But on the other hand, the same God looked at a blatant, caught-in-the-act kind of sin and poured out His grace and mercy on the sinner. Why? Because He is Elohim, and He is Yahweh.

God's bigness and nearness can be seen all throughout Scripture, which is why it's critical for Moses to point out the contrast at the very beginning, as it was evidenced in creation. From the opening chapters of God's Word, He shows us all of Himself. God is Elohim. He is more powerful and set apart than we can ever imagine. But He is also Yahweh. He is more intimate and near to us than we can ever imagine.

God isn't one or the other. He wasn't Elohim on day one of creation and Yahweh on day two. He wasn't Elohim in the Old Testament and Yahweh in the New Testament.

 Listen to "Everlasting God" by Brenton Brown from the *Creation Unraveled* playlist, available at *threadsmedia. com/creationunraveled*.

He isn't half Elohim and half Yahweh. He is fully both, all the time. It's critical that we understand this, because we have a tendency to emphasize and relate to one aspect of God's character at the expense of the other. And when we do that, there is no lighter way to describe it than as idolatry.

ARE YOU AN "ELOHIM" OR A "YAHWEH" PERSON?

Some of us are tempted to think about and relate to God as Yahweh and completely ignore that He is Elohim. Others of us relate to the transcendent, big Elohim but can't begin to connect with our intimate, near Yahweh. The danger is that if the god you worship is just Elohim or just Yahweh, then you aren't worshiping the God of the Bible, because that God is both. Instead, you're worshiping a god you created, and you might as well be bowing down to a wooden statue.

Which way do you lean? Have you bent so far to one direction or the other that the god you worship isn't the God of the Bible? If you're unsure which way you err, here are a few diagnostic statements to help you figure it out.

1. How to tell if you overemphasize Elohim:

When you picture God, is He powerful, righteous, and filled with hatred for sin? Well you're right, those are all aspects of His character. Undoubtedly God is powerful, righteous, and just, but here are some clues to see if you lean too heavily on worshiping only the Elohim traits of God:

- Does your interaction with God reflect Him as someone who at best tolerates you and at worst waits for you to mess up so He can punish you? *When I was living in sin - YES*

- Is it difficult for you to understand God's forgiveness and grace? When you repent of sin, do you feel like you're still waiting for God's punishment? Or do you find yourself looking for ways to make it up to Him so He doesn't disown you? *I use to wait for his punishment - disgusted by me*

- Is your general view of God that He is frustrated with your failure and <u>disappointed by your feeble attempts</u> to pursue holiness?

- When you fail, do you find yourself running from God instead of running to Him? *Yes & No*

If the god you worship never comforts you, picks you up and holds you, or whispers in your ear how much he loves you and how he's crazy about you, you're worshiping a god of your own making. If you don't see God as the safest Person to turn to in times of failure, distress, suffering or sin, then you're focused on His bigness and have forgotten His nearness.

 Watch the *Creation Unraveled* video "The Bigness and Nearness of God," available at *threadsmedia.com/creationunraveled*.

2. How to tell if you overemphasize Yahweh:

When you picture God, is He like a loving dad? Do you think of Jesus as a kind, gentle friend who's always there to comfort you and tell you how much He loves you? These are true aspects of God's character, however here are some clues that your heart is leaning toward idolatry by isolating these characteristics:

- When you read passages of the Old Testament like Habakkuk 1 that describe God destroying entire cities and the men, women, and children in them, do you think to yourself, *That's not my God?* *No*

- Do you make light of your sin? In the midst of temptation, do you think, *I know this is wrong, but I know my God will forgive me?* *No*
But I did think He would never leave me – see me through

- Do you find your heart responding to sermons or songs that celebrate God's love, but notice yourself disengaging from sermons or songs that emphasize God's holiness or justice? *No*

- Does the concept of hell make you uncomfortable?
Makes me SAD – sometimes scared

If the god you worship never challenges you, never interjects and demands his will over yours, or never forces you to change, you've created a god in your image. If God never challenges you or demands His will over yours, I guarantee you it's not because you're completely conformed to His image and there's no more work left to do in your heart. Rather, the overemphasis of God's nearness has blinded you to His justice and power, leaving you comfortable where you are and in your sin. God loves you no matter where you are, but He doesn't want you to stay there. The God of the Bible will always challenge you and demand His will over yours. When we fail to see God in His entirety, we fail to love Him.

CASE STUDIES

Coming to terms with the complexity of God's character was a game changer for me in my relationship with God. Over the years, there have been two areas of my life that I've never understood. When I say never, I mean *never*. I've never understood why Christians act the way they do, or why I act the way I do. I'll tell you about me in a minute. But first, I finally understood that when godly people act a certain way over and over again, they do so because they've embraced one aspect of God's character and dismissed the other.

I see this all the time when I'm counseling people. For the record, I'm the world's worst counselor. People come into my office and tell me about all the ways they're sinning. Then when they ask me for guidance, I look at them and, with great wisdom and insight, I say, "Why don't you stop sinning?" That's my counseling technique—telling them to stop. And I can't tell you how many people say, "No, I'm going to keep doing it." And when I ask why, their response is that God loves them and will always forgive them. But in my mind, because I'm an Elohim guy, I'm thinking, "Don't you know that God can kill you?" These are incredible counseling skills, I know.

One guy who came to me for counseling seemed on the surface to be all you would imagine a good husband to be. But in reality, the choices he made reflected the opposite. He left his wife and abandoned his family, and his wife asked me to meet with him. I tried the pastoral approach first. I loved on the guy, listened to his story, and tried to understand why he was doing what he was doing. He told me he didn't want to come home, he didn't want to end the affair he was having, and he had no desire to restore his relationship with his wife. He was done with his marriage and family.

In my efforts to counsel him, I asked him if he understood what the covenant of marriage means, and what it means that Jesus said, "What God has joined together, no man should break apart" (Matthew 19:6). He responded with a, "Yeah, I get that." So I asked him a simple question: "Are you going to repent? Do you want to get this right with your wife and with Jesus?" He looked me in the eye and said no.

At that point I took off my kind pastoral hat and put on my Old Testament prophet hat. I explained to him that he was claiming the name of Jesus but wasn't repenting, which meant one of two things was happening in his life. Option one was that he wasn't saved, because Scripture states very clearly that he who is born of God doesn't continue in sin, and he was choosing sin. I told him that if that was the case, then if something happened to him when he walked out that door, he would go to hell. Option two was that he *was* saved, in which case if he didn't repent, then the discipline of God would come crashing in on his life. I've been there, and no one wants that.

Sadly, my friend ignored the Word of God and cruised on with his life. Why? Because he was convinced that it didn't matter what he did. That no matter what, God would forgive him. To some extent, that's true. The nature of God's grace is such that He's willing to forgive anything we've ever done, no matter how bad, but that doesn't give us a license to sin. Our God, in His bigness and nearness, wants our love for Him to produce obedience.

In studying Genesis 1 and 2, I came to terms with something I've always struggled with—confidently believing God loves me. I can say it to myself and preach it from the pulpit, but I don't always believe that truth. One of the first thoughts that crossed my mind when I was diagnosed with cancer in 2005 was that I deserved cancer and that it

Yahweh is often referred to as the *tetragrammaton*, which means "four letters," because the transliteration of the Hebrew is YHWH.

made sense that God would punish me in that way. The reason I wrestle so deeply with this truth is because I have embraced my God as Elohim, but I haven't embraced Him as Yahweh.

I'm crazy about my children. I love them in ways I can't articulate. I emotionally love them. I love them passionately and with a servant's heart. I love them completely and fully. My sons and my daughter couldn't do anything to change how much I love them. Yet Scripture, which I would give my life for and I believe every word of, tells me, "Matt, you know how much you love your children? Your God, your Heavenly Daddy, loves you even more than that." But still, I deeply struggle to believe it.

The first two chapters of Genesis help me understand that when I embrace God as Elohim but ignore that He's also Yahweh, I'm not loving God the way He desires. Because, you see, you can't really love people if you pick and choose what you want to love about them. In order to love people genuinely, you have to love everything about them. The same is true for our love of God.

You may be content with the version of God you have in your mind. You may find it uncomfortable or unnecessary to engage with all aspects of His character. You may think that your love for Him is simple and that you don't need to know everything about Him in order to love Him. However, we must recognize that we can't truly claim to love God if we refuse to embrace all that He is revealing about Himself to us.

Consider, for example, if I come home one night and my wife, Jennifer, has a candlelit dinner on the table and a sitter for the kids. We sit down, and she looks at me with tears in her eyes and says, "Matt, we need to talk. There is a part of me that you either don't know about or you've been ignoring. But I want you to know, love, and embrace all of me. It might be hard, but here it is. This is who I really am."

As she is about to reveal to me an aspect of her character that I need to see, my heart starts pounding. I get scared. I look at her and think, *You know, I'm comfortable with the Jen I already know. I'm not sure I want to see this other aspect of her. The Jen I've spent the last 15 years with is good enough for me.* So I look at her, dry her tears, and say, "No thanks. I'd rather not know."

We would never call that love. Yet we do that to God all the time. We're content to ignore aspects of His character, but we still claim to love Him. For us to fully love Him, we have to love all of Him. Embrace all of Him. Study all of Him. Worship all of Him. He is Elohim and Yahweh, transcendent and intimate, big and near.

 "Because you have made the LORD—my refuge, the Most High—your dwelling place, no harm will come to you; no plague will come near your tent. For He will give His angels orders concerning you, to protect you in all your ways" (Psalm 91:9-11).

Are you an "Elohim" person or a "Yahweh" person? Why do you prefer to relate with God that way?

Praise God - I am both but I lean towards Elohim more.

- I think I was taught more about "Elohim".

Is it difficult for you to value both aspects of God's character? Why or why not?

No - As I get older & understand how much He loves me - I see him as both Elohim & Yahweh

At what times in your life have you seen the Yahweh aspect of God's nature?

In times of heart ache & in my quiet time I feel his nearness - I feel so drawn to Him

At what times in your life have you seen the Elohim aspect of God's nature?

When I was dabbling in SIN - looking back on that time in my life - I see consequences for my choices YET His Mercy.

Leading a group? It's the way to go.
Find extra questions and teaching
tools in the leader kit, available at
threadsmedia.com/creationunraveled.

Think back through the Yahweh times and consider how God also displayed Himself as Elohim during those times.

He was being "Elohim" in my Spouses life –

Then think back through the Elohim times and consider how God displayed Himself as Yahweh at the same time, keeping in mind that God is always both.

He was still with Me & full of such Mercy – when I ultimately deserved punishment!

How has your bent toward God's Elohim or Yahweh character traits affected your relationship with Him? How has it affected your relationships with others?

When I was Younger – I feared Him I was Scared of punishment –
I Need to examine "the god" I am presenting to my Kids.

What evidence do you see of both God's Elohim and Yahweh characteristics in how Jesus related to people while He was on earth? Give some examples from specific stories in the Gospels.

Judus
Paul
Mary / Martha

IN YOUR DEVOTION TIME THIS WEEK, make a list of all the places that reveal God as Elohim and all the places that reveal God as Yahweh. Try to find practical ways you can live out the truths in those verses.

Share what you've learned in this week's session with your spouse and/or a close friend. Ask them if they think you're an "Elohim" person or a "Yahweh" person, and ask for reasons why they think so.

Search through the Bible and find verses that specifically reveal God's "bigness" (e.g. Psalm 91:9-11) and verses that specifically reveal His "nearness" (e.g. Psalm 91:14-16). Find three or four passages of Scripture for both and memorize them. Apply them in the areas of your life where you're tempted to only identify with one aspect of God over the other.

2 Chron - When Gods people cried out to him - He would resue them
Then at times He would send an Army to destroy them for their Sin - Have the enemy Kill them or strike them w/ disease.

Practical Ways to live out truths:
- Worship Only God
- Pray Continually
- Eliminate anything that gets in the way of teaching kids about God or learning who he is!

THE GOODNESS OF SIN VS. THE GOODNESS OF GOD

GENESIS 3

SESSION THREE

"Then the woman saw that the tree was good for food and delightful to look at, and that it was desirable for obtaining wisdom. So she took some of its fruit and ate it; she also gave some to her husband, who was with her, and he ate it" (Genesis 3:6).

As we continue our progress through the Book of Genesis, I (Halim) need to warn you about what's to come. This session marks the beginning of a four-session look into sin. In a study that's only seven sessions long, we're going to spend more than half of them looking at the concept and origin of sin. Why? Because, simply put, unless we understand the gravity of sin, we can't cherish the gospel.[i]

The gospel is the good news that when Christ rose from the grave, He conquered both sin and death. As Christians, we believe that the death and resurrection of Jesus is the single most important event in all of human history. It should mean everything for the believer. After all, Paul said that if Christ hasn't been raised, our faith is worthless, we're still in our sins, and we're to be pitied.[1] But if we're honest with ourselves, when we think about Jesus' death and resurrection, we may not feel like it's the most important thing that's ever happened to us. Sadly, it's often reduced to a once-a-year celebration in April when we dress a bit more fancy for church. Many other things compete for the title of "greatest thing that's happened in our lives."

Consider this: What if later today we turn on the evening news and discover that scientists have found a cure for cancer—a vaccine that cures any type of cancer, regardless of what stage it's in? The world would erupt in celebration. Cell phone networks would shut down because of the number of calls being attempted. From living rooms to hospital beds, there would be tears of joy and lots of celebration.

We live in a world where most people know someone who battles cancer, has survived it, or has lost the fight with it. Many of us have seen first-hand the number of deaths it brings. Matt was diagnosed with cancer in 2005, and my mom passed away from sarcoma in 2008. Because we live in a world where there's no doubt about the calamity of cancer, if we discovered a cure, the world would celebrate it as one of the greatest moments in human history.

So why don't we cherish the death and resurrection of Jesus as truly the greatest moment in our history? Because while we may fully relate to the physical devastation cancer brings, many of us fail to grasp the fullness of the physical and spiritual devastation brought on by sin. News of a cure for cancer won't impress us very much if we don't consider cancer a serious problem. Likewise, we won't treasure the death and resurrection of Jesus if we don't view sin as a devastating problem in the world.

Jesus' death and resurrection was the greatest solution, the greatest cure, and the greatest rescue that a world enveloped in sin could hope for. It was the only thing that could've made a difference in our hopeless reality. But we can't cherish it the way it's

---

 1. "And if Christ has not been raised, your faith is worthless; you are still in your sins. Therefore, those who have fallen asleep in Christ have also perished. If we have put our hope in Christ for this life only, we should be pitied more than anyone" (1 Corinthians 15:17-19).

meant to be cherished if we refuse to see sin for what it really is. If our perception of sin is deluded, our worship of God is shallow.

For this reason, understanding the next several chapters of Genesis and everything they teach us about sin is foundational to our appreciation for the Person and work of Jesus Christ.

Up to this point in our walk through Genesis, we've read about how God created the world. He made everything, and at the pinnacle of His creating, He made humanity. God brought forth the human race, male and female, and He gave them the highest dignity of all creation by creating them in His own image. He prepared the entire world for His children's entrance, like any good father would do.

We see this theme of preparation reflected today when couples get the news that they're going to have a child. My wife, Angela, and I experienced one of the greatest moments of our lives in October 2007 when we welcomed our first born, Malachi. We prepared for his birth during the nine months of pregnancy. We got him a crib and a changing table, and we painted his room. I learned about things like Bumbo™ chairs, aspirators, and Baby Björn® carriers. Everything was ready for him. And when he was born, and I held him for the first time, the only words I found to express my feelings toward him were these: "Everything I have is yours."

This is the picture we see of God in Genesis 1 and 2. God gave Adam paradise; He told him that everything He made was there for him to enjoy. He told him, "The sun, moon, and stars are there for you. Every beast of the earth, every creature in the seas, every bird in the sky I made for you. This is for you to have and take care of. Enjoy all that I've made, because I had you in mind when it came into being."

As if that weren't enough, God gave the first humans something of infinite value—something that couldn't be paralleled with any other gift bestowed in creation. God gave them Himself. Bearing His image, Adam and Eve freely and intimately walked with God in the garden. They had a fellowship with the Creator that we can only long for.

Can you wrap your mind around what that was like? I can't comprehend what heights of perfection existed in the garden with God, but I know for certain that something inside me longs to experience the ultimate joy and contentment that was Adam and Eve's reality. We spend our lives searching to regain what they had in the garden of Eden. The canyons of that goodness must run deeper than we can imagine if our souls still feel the sting of its loss. But there was a time, as we see in the early chapters of Genesis, when we had everything we could've dreamed of.

God offered Adam everything, even Himself, but with one prohibition:

> "The Lord God took the man and placed him in the garden of Eden to work it and watch over it. And the Lord God commanded the man, 'You are free to eat from any tree of the garden, but you must not eat from the tree of the knowledge of good and evil, for on the day you eat from it, you will certainly die'" (Genesis 2:15-17).

That was it. Surely that one guideline wasn't too hard to obey, right? It's like second nature for me to avoid fruit! And I imagine there were plenty of other fruit-bearing trees in the garden they could eat from. So what made this particular command so difficult to follow?

For those of you with smaller children, you've probably seen this play out before your very eyes at home. When you tell children not to do something, they become consumed with the very thing you ask them not to do, and it's just a matter of time before they do it. If you have older children, you may tell them not to touch this or that, and the first thing out of their mouths is, "Why?"

God didn't give Adam the details as to why he wasn't supposed to eat from the tree, did He? God only told him not to eat from the tree and what the immediate consequence would be if anyone disobeyed Him. God didn't teach Adam about the theology behind the tree of the knowledge of good and evil. God didn't explain that eating its fruit would usher in every measure of horror to His beautiful and spotless creation. God didn't tell him that suffering, oppression, chaos, and wars would be some of the results of disobedience to that single command. God didn't tell him that eating the fruit would banish him and the entire lineage of humanity from His presence and into eternal punishment. God simply said he would die.

Don't you think knowing those consequences would've been helpful information? Surely it would've changed things if God had said, "Adam and Eve, if you eat of this fruit, you will watch your children murder each other, and their sons and daughters will watch their parents die slowly from disease and famine. Your act of rebellion will be the source of every sin and misery that will occur throughout history." I like to think that information would've helped me in my decision making if I was faced with their choice. I could've hit up another tree for an apple, or maybe I would've had some vegetables instead. Those are some extreme consequences to risk for a piece of fruit.

If God had given Adam and Eve more details about why His command was so important to keep, then maybe they would've responded differently to the serpent. When Satan found them in the garden and said, "That tree looks good, why don't you enjoy some of its fruit?," perhaps our first parents would've sidestepped the land mine and said, "No, thanks."

God could've set Adam and Eve up to withstand the ploy of Satan by giving them more information, so why didn't He? If God gave them an exhaustive list of the "whys" for not eating the fruit He commanded them not to eat, what would their obedience have been rooted in? Cost-benefit analysis? Their own wisdom? Their desire for self-preservation?

God wanted their obedience to be rooted in His wisdom and logic, not their own. He wanted His goodness and faithfulness to be sufficient. Had He given them more information, they might have acted differently, but it would have been because God made a convincing argument and they trusted themselves—not because they trusted God supremely.

Do we trust God enough to obey Him without knowing the details surrounding a particular command or circumstance? Or will we only bend our knee when His commands make sense or line up with what we think ought to happen anyway?

God wants us to trust in His goodness. From the very core of who we are, He wants us to know that He's a good Father who desires to give us every good and perfect gift (James 1:17). He also wants us to trust that when He withholds things from us, it's only those things that would cause us harm.

Have you ever wanted someone to do something important for you, but for whatever reason you couldn't explain to them why? You tell them, "I really need you to do this; I can't explain why, but I need you to trust me." This type of request eliminates all room for ulterior motives; it's simply rooted in trust.

God desires obedient hearts more than obedient hands. This is why He was so displeased with the Pharisees throughout the New Testament; they had it backwards. Sure, they did all the right things through their actions, but their hearts didn't trust God any more than people who publicly renounced Him. Rather than seeing God as an object of worship, the Pharisees saw Him more like a promissory note (that would eventually pay out big).

When it comes to sin, the central issue isn't the disobedience of the hands; it's the distrust of the heart. Usually we're so focused on our behavior that we exhaust our energy trying to act better, while completely neglecting the affections of our hearts. We sin, so we make a promise to God that we'll never make that mistake again, only to repeat the cycle soon after our vow.

 Listen to "Leaving Eden" by Brandon Heath from the *Creation Unraveled* playlist, available at *threadsmedia. com/creationunraveled*.

But the sin that primarily concerns God is our lack of trust in Him. When we experience failure, we shouldn't focus our attention on behaving better. Instead, we should beg God to reveal to us how we failed to trust in His goodness so that we may believe and be changed from the inside out. Our obedience to Him should be rooted in trust—the same trust He wanted Adam and Eve to experience in the garden.

A STRATEGIC DECEPTION

This may be the first time you've considered the connection between the heart and sin, or maybe it's something you're familiar with. Regardless, someone else knows how crucial trust is in the fight against sin better than you and I ever will. That someone is Satan. He knows that if he can get us to question God's goodness, then he has us where he wants us. Distrust is a vulnerable weakness that allows him to strike a shattering blow.

> **"Now the serpent was more crafty than any beast of the field which the LORD God had made. And he said to the woman, 'Indeed, has God said, "You shall not eat from any tree of the garden"?' The woman said to the serpent, 'From the fruit of the trees of the garden we may eat; but from the fruit of the tree which is in the middle of the garden, God has said, "You shall not eat from it or touch it, or you will die."' The serpent said to the woman, 'You surely will not die! For God knows that in the day you eat from it your eyes will be opened, and you will be like God, knowing good and evil'" (Genesis 3:1-5, NASB).**

Satan spoke to Adam and Eve through the serpent in this passage. The first thing the text tells us about the serpent is that he's more crafty than any other creature God created. This craftiness is a clue to pay attention not only to what the serpent says but also to his motivations for what he says. With that in mind, let's look again at what the serpent said to Eve in verse 1:

> **"Indeed, has God said, 'You shall not eat from any tree of the garden'?"**

We know from the apostle Paul that every word in Scripture is inspired by God and useful for teaching (2 Timothy 3:16), and that truth is demonstrated through a subtle word used by the serpent—*indeed*. I can almost hear the serpent utter that word with a tone of condescension, giving us the sense that Satan didn't deny what God said; instead he mocked Him: "Are you kidding? Did God really say you can't eat that? Is He so selfish that He won't let you have something that's good for you?"

Satan didn't stop with mockery. He added to his deception by twisting God's words just enough to fan the flame of doubt in the hearts of Adam and Eve. Remember, God told

---

Watch the *Creation Unraveled* video "The Goodness of Sin vs. the Goodness of God" available at *threadsmedia.com/creationunraveled.*

them they could eat of every tree in the garden except the tree of the knowledge of good and evil (Genesis 2:16-17). But Satan slithers over to them and says, "So, God told you that you can't eat from any of these trees, huh?"

Satan cunningly tried to convince Adam and Eve that God's withholding *something* from them was the same as withholding *everything* from them. How could Adam and Eve be so foolish as to fall for that trick? Isn't that how we feel sometimes, though? God doesn't give us that one thing we really want, so instead of recognizing everything we do have and praising Him for it, we feel like He hasn't given us anything and wallow in our self pity.

This reminds me of the blockbuster movie *Inception*. In the film, the main characters act as thieves, breaking into people's dreams to interact with them in their subconscious. Their main objective is to plant ideas so deeply into the minds of their targets that they believe the ideas were their own. Once the ideas are planted, the targets carry out the desires of the thieves under the guise that they're doing so of their own volition. In the garden, Satan planted his own lie into the minds of Adam and Eve. He made them believe that God wasn't who He claimed to be. Satan planted the seed of doubt that maybe God had been lying to them and wasn't good at all. Satan set them up to carry out his plan to separate God from His most prized possession—His children.

Satan, though evil and horrific, has strengths that he utilizes to the fullest measure. One of those is his trickery. Instead of attacking Adam and Eve with a statement or command, he posed a deceptive question. His first move was to carefully and strategically lay the trap, which shifted the attitude of the first humans' hearts. Then he attacked with his lie. The heart must be infiltrated first, then the mind will believe even the most blatant lie: "You will not surely die."

Only after Adam and Eve wrestled with the possibility that God might not be good could Satan challenge the trustworthiness of God's word. If we truly believed that God is good, then we would cling to every single word in the Bible and obey it as if our lives depended on it. But we wonder, we hesitate, and we leave just enough room for Satan to push us over the edge.

Satan knows what's most crucial to destroy. He didn't bring into question God's existence because the evidence to the contrary was too strong. Instead, he raised issue with God's goodness, and he forced Adam and Eve (like he forces us) to ask themselves, *Is God really good?*

Isn't that the question the world asks?

"If God is so good, then why do people suffer?"

"If God is so good, then why does He allow tragedy to happen?"

"If God is so good, then why is there injustice everywhere I look?"

Satan hasn't changed his tactics all that much, has he? But why should he, when we see how effective he was in Genesis 3? In the garden of Eden, Satan attacked the goodness of God's motives in His command to not eat from the tree. He manipulated and deceived them into believing they couldn't trust God and needed to take ownership of their lives if they wanted what was truly best for themselves.

Satan wove into their subconscious the lie that if they obeyed God, they would be missing out on something better. He told them there was more out there for them, but they would never experience it if they settled for what God promised them. Oh, the irony of this trickery! Satan caused the first humans to be so convinced they were missing out on something that humanity eventually lost everything.

THE LIE THAT KEEPS ON LYING

The lie about God's goodness went straight into Adam and Eve's hearts. It went into my heart, your heart, and the heart of every man and woman who has and will ever live. And as you've probably noticed, this lie isn't dormant within us. Satan's lie prompted Adam and Eve to rebel against God's command, and it prompts us to do the same even today. For you it may look like this:

"I know the Bible says I need to fight for my marriage and not get a divorce, but a divorce sure would make life easier." Or: *"I know God commands me to forgive, not to hold a grudge or seek revenge against this person, but I refuse to let go of my anger."* Or: *"I know God's Word says I need to be generous and give cheerfully, but if I give this much and not that much, then I'd be able to . . . "*

This is temptation at its finest. We know God's commands. We hear them preached and read them in the Word, and we know obeying His commands is supposed to be the means by which we find our greatest joy—life spent with Him. *But . . .* We're too familiar with that three-letter word, aren't we? Over and over again, we say to ourselves, *I know God's command, but what if . . . "* Deep down inside of ourselves, we believe the lie that we can't trust God, at least not fully. When Satan confronted Adam and Eve in the garden, we were introduced to the thought that God alone isn't sufficient, and we bought that lie hook, line, and sinker. We believe that obedience to Him will cost us more than it's worth and we'll never be happy.

 Listen to "Broken Hallelujah" by Mandisa from the *Creation Unraveled* playlist, available at *threadsmedia. com/creationunraveled.*

Sadly, believing this lie is what truly jeopardizes our happiness. Being obedient to God's will is supposed to be what brings us fulfillment and joy. He created us, so if anyone knows how to make us happy, it's Him. But when Satan peppers our view of God's goodness with doubt, we question His motives and take matters into our own hands. *How could a good God withhold that goodness from you?* he whispers. *If He withholds anything from you, it's the same as withholding everything from you.* The serpent's assertion to Eve wreaked havoc in the heart of humanity.

THE HUMAN STAIN

The triumph of Satan to deceive God's children into doubting His goodness is the root of every evil in the world. This great lie is the "human stain" we all bear, to borrow a phrase from Philip Roth's novel *The Human Stain*. In a sermon on Genesis 3 titled "Paradise in Crisis," author and pastor Tim Keller mentioned the following passage from Roth's book. Notice the picture of sin Roth paints through the voice of one of the book's female characters:

> "It's in everyone . . . Inherent. Defining. The stain is there before its mark. Without the sign it is there. The stain so intrinsic that it doesn't require a mark. The stain that precedes disobedience, that encompasses disobedience and perplexes all explanation and understanding. It's why all the cleansing is a joke. A barbaric joke at that. The fantasy of purity is appalling. It's insane. What is the quest to purify, if not more impurity?"[2]

Sin is in everyone; it's inescapable. It's a stain smeared over each of us, and it's visible before we ever act disobediently. As Roth's character observes, the thought of being able to cleanse ourselves from the stain of sin is a malicious and appalling fantasy, because it's impossible. In fact, the more we try out of our own efforts to eradicate sin from our lives, the more we continue in our pattern to sin. Apart from God's intervention, we're trapped in this cycle forever.

Let's keep this in mind as we return to our story in Genesis. Satan planted his lie, and then what happened?

> **"Then the woman saw that the tree was good for food and delightful to look at, and that it was desirable for obtaining wisdom. So she took some of its fruit and ate it; she also gave some to her husband, who was with her, and he ate it" (Genesis 3:6).**

When Eve stopped seeing God as good, she started seeing the fruit of the tree as good instead. Isn't this the case with anything we're prohibited to have? When our hearts

2. Philip Roth, *The Human Stain: A Novel American Trilogy* (New York: Vintage International, 2001), 242.

stop seeing God as good, those less satisfying things in our world become much more desirable, and we're tempted to replace Him with them.

Before Satan's temptation, Adam and Eve relied on God as the source of all goodness, and they lived in truth. But the great danger of sin is that it never shows you its true face. Sin is always evil masquerading as good. Instead of living in truth, we live in deception. Consider author Paul David Tripp's imagery:

> "Sin lives in a costume; that's why it is so hard to recognize. The fact that sin looks so good is one of the things that makes it so bad. In order for it to do its evil work, it must present itself as something that is anything but evil. Life in a fallen world is like attending the ultimate masquerade party. Impatient yelling wears the costume of zeal for the truth. Lust can masquerade as a love for beauty. Gossip does its evil work by living in the costume of concern and prayer. Craving for power and control wears the mask of biblical leadership. Fear of man gets dressed up as a servant heart. The pride of always being right masquerades as a love for biblical wisdom. Evil simply doesn't present itself as evil, which is part of its draw. You'll never understand sin's sleight of hand until you acknowledge that the DNA of sin is deception. Now, what this means personally is that as sinners we are all very committed and gifted self-swindlers. We are too skilled at looking at our own wrong and seeing good."[3]

So, deceived by sin's mask of goodness, Eve took fruit from the tree and ate it. Contrary to popular belief, Adam wasn't elsewhere in the garden practicing godliness, oblivious to the fact that Eve was throwing everything away for a piece of fruit. Nor was he unaware of what he was doing when he ate the fruit Eve gave him. Scripture tells us Adam was by Eve's side during the serpent's entire pitch:

> **"So she took some of its fruit and ate it; she also gave some to *her husband, who was with her*, and he ate it" (Genesis 3:6, emphasis added).**

Not a shining moment of biblical manhood for Adam, was it? While Satan questioned the goodness of their Creator and spat lies into the heart of Adam's bride, Adam looked on and, through inaction, supported everything that happened. Eve ate, and Adam followed right behind her. They ate fruit. Such a simple act. When you look at it on paper, it doesn't seem all that evil, does it? It isn't like Adam and Eve went on a killing spree and murdered all of the animals. No, it was the simple act of eating—a seemingly small act of disobedience—that carried with it unimaginably grave consequences.

---

3. Paul David Tripp, *Whiter Than Snow: Meditations on Sin and Mercy* (Wheaton, Illinois: Crossway, 2008), 32.

SESSION THREE CREATION UNRAVELED

THE OFFENDED CREATOR

"Let me never forget that the heinousness of sin lies not so much in the nature of the sin committed, as in the greatness of the Person sinned against." —*The Valley of Vision*[4]

Consider all of the small, seemingly inconsequential sins we write off as no big deal because they don't seem to affect much. The way we see it, our efforts should be focused on eradicating our "bigger" sins first, right? Wrong. When we allow ourselves to view sin through the lens of how it hurts us or those around us, we miss the point of sin's gravity altogether. Sin isn't severe because of the effect it has on us; it's unimaginably severe because of the greatness of Who it offends. An offense against an infinite God is infinitely severe.

Think about a "small" sin you've committed, like one of those infamous little white lies. What happens when you lie to your friend or spouse? Perhaps an argument unfolds and you deal with conflict, but unless your lie is extreme, there's typically little consequence on your life as a whole. Now, let's say you lie to a police officer or a judge, someone with more authority than your friend. What happens then? You could go to jail for lying to someone with that kind of authority. The sin was the same, but the consequence increased. And what if you lied to the President of the United States? That could be considered treason, which has been known to warrant a death sentence.

We're still talking about the same "little" lie, so why does it bring such a varied array of consequences? Because even in the secular world, there's an understanding that the act is only as significant as the person who's offended. When we sin, even in small, seemingly harmless ways, we offend the greatest and most powerful Person who's ever entered the landscape of history and who created it all—God. For this reason, we should see all our sins as infinitely horrific.

EYES WIDE OPEN

The sin that started them all was an act of disobedience to God's command, rooted in a distrust of God's goodness. At Satan's prompting, our first parents belittled God by claiming that while He may be many things, good is not one of them. What was the consequence of such an offense? Actually, the first sin carried many consequences. But for now, let's look at one in particular.

> **"Then the eyes of both of them were opened, and they knew they were naked; so they sewed fig leaves together and made loincloths for themselves. Then the man and his wife heard the sound of the Lord God walking in the garden at the time of the evening breeze, and they hid themselves from the Lord God among the trees of the garden. So the Lord God called out to the**

4. Arthur Bennett, ed., *The Valley of Vision: A Collection of Puritan Prayers & Devotions* (Carlisle, Pennsylvania: The Banner of Truth Trust, Eighth Printing, 2009), 79.

man and said to him, 'Where are you?' And he said, 'I heard You in the garden and I was afraid because I was naked, so I hid'" (Genesis 3:7-10).

Adam and Eve's eyes were opened, and they became aware of their nakedness. In an attempt to cover their shame, they made clothes out of fig leaves. Then when God came to walk with them in the garden, they hid from Him, because, according to Adam, they didn't want Him to see their nakedness. But they had always been naked.

Before they exchanged the goodness of God for the goodness of sin, their nakedness didn't matter because they felt clothed. They were covered with God's goodness. They were unashamed, secure, and provided for. When they disobeyed God and questioned His goodness, they lost their covering of glory, leaving them feeling naked and exposed. At the heart of it, we see that sin was a great exchange Adam and Eve made. Paul describes this type of exchange in Romans 1:

> "For though they knew God, they did not glorify Him as God or show gratitude. Instead, their thinking became nonsense, and their senseless minds were darkened. Claiming to be wise, they became fools and exchanged the glory of the immortal God for images resembling mortal man, birds, four-footed animals, and reptiles" (Romans 1:21-23).

Through a series of comparisons, Paul described the great distance between people and God. We exchanged the glory of the *incorruptible* God for images in the forms of *corruptible* man, birds, and animals. In this great exchange, we flipped upside down the created order that God established. Instead of being subjected to God our Creator and ruling over creation, we subjected ourselves to a created thing—a serpent—in an attempt to place our authority over God's authority.

Before Adam and Eve believed Satan's lie, they felt no shame. They didn't have anything to hide and could be completely vulnerable before God and one another. They experienced the satisfaction of being both fully known and fully loved. After they sinned, however, they felt shameful and guilty. The clothing of God's goodness, acceptance, glory, and purity is what enabled them to stand before Him without shame or guilt. When it was removed, the thought of being fully known became horrifying.

Can you relate to those feelings? What if someone you deeply care for learned how you really are, deep down inside? What if they knew the secret thoughts that run through your mind every day? Would they still love you, or would they abandon you? God created us to be fully known and fully loved. But in our fallen state, we've convinced ourselves that the only way we can be loved is if we're *not* fully known. In the innermost parts of our being, we believe it's impossible for anyone to know the depths of who we are and still love us. So, we hide.

The next time you wonder why you feel the way you do, when you feel a sense of loss or a sense that something is deeply wrong with you, know that it's a memory of the glory, greatness, and paradise lost long ago.

AN INSUFFICIENT COVERING

The thought of two people trying to cover their nakedness with little fig leaves is borderline comical. As was their attempt to hide from an omnipresent God. Did they really think God wouldn't find them? We chuckle, but in reality we have an abundance of fig leaves we try to hide behind. We often play "the covering game" to present the most acceptable versions of ourselves to the world.

The majority of our time is spent attempting to cover our nakedness, and we're unbelievably good at it. Since hiding who we truly are is the only way we think we'll be loved, we pretend to be someone else. *I need to be someone worth loving, so I'll find a way to make that happen. I'll cover myself with my own fig leaves and cling to them like life vests.* We have a desperate need to control what people know about us because we're naked and ashamed. This is evident in our everyday, mundane actions as well as our most significant ones.

For example, have you ever gone to the restroom in your office building and skipped the hand washing because you were in a hurry? If someone was in there, though, you'd wash your hands so they wouldn't think you're filthy. Or what about when a coworker asks you how you're doing? Without even thinking about it you probably reply, "Good!" Perhaps a guy you're interested in asks you out on a date and says he'll pick you up at your apartment. What's the first thing you do? Deep clean the apartment so he won't see how undisciplined you are in day-to-day life. Some of you didn't find out how unkempt your spouse was until after you got married because they hid it from you.

We are terrified of being known, so we try to cover ourselves. But is it working? You may be successful or loved, but do you still feel naked? Do people truly know you? And for that matter, do you truly know yourself? Some of the most successful people on earth are the ones who have done the best job sewing their fig leaves together.

Sadly, trying to cover ourselves is a tragic waste of time. Our "fig leaves" don't help the exposure of our souls any more than tape helps a severed limb. Even after Adam and Eve broke their communion with God, they were still dependent on Him to sufficiently cover them. And out of His goodness—the goodness Adam and Eve failed to trust—He did just that. At the height of their rebellion and rejection, God gave them a more durable and protective covering than fig leaves:

> "The LORD God made clothing out of skins for Adam and his wife, and He clothed them" (Genesis 3:21).

Don't miss the fact that the garments God made for Adam and Eve were made from skin. Blood had to be shed for them to have a better covering. A life had to be taken. In the midst of humanity's most tragic moment, we see a hint at redemption—a reference to the sacrificial system of the tabernacle and the temple, and ultimately to the atoning work of Jesus Himself on the cross. Initially God covered His children with clothing, but eventually He would cover them with righteousness.

PARADISE LOST

As another consequence of their rebellion, Adam and Eve were banished from paradise:

> "The LORD God said, 'Since man has become like one of Us, knowing good and evil, he must not reach out, take from the tree of life, eat, and live forever.' So the LORD God sent him away from the garden of Eden to work the ground from which he was taken. He drove man out and stationed the cherubim and the flaming, whirling sword east of the garden of Eden to guard the way to the tree of life" (Genesis 3:22-24).

Here we see the greatest loss of humanity as a result of the fall. The garden was where God and humanity walked freely together, in intimacy and relationship. However, when they listened to the serpent, they lost that communion, and God placed His cherubim outside the garden's entrance. In the words of Old Testament scholar Derek Kidner, "Every detail of this verse [verse 24], with its flame and sword and the turning every way, actively excludes the sinner."[5]

We became God's enemies, and the guards' presence indicates the impossibility of a human-initiated reestablishment of relationship with God. Never again can we, on our own initiative, reenter the state of Eden. No matter how many fig leaves we have, or how elaborate they are, we'll never be able to cover ourselves adequately. For that, we're dependent on Him.

If we'll ever commune with God again like we did in Eden, it's up to Him to make it happen. The good news is, He's going to make it happen. He's already started the process. That's precisely what the rest of the Bible is about—the relentless pursuit of reconciliation with man forged by God. Throughout the rest of the Bible, God says time and again,

---

5. Derek Kidner, *Genesis: An Introduction and Commentary, Vol. 1.* (Downers Grove, Illinois: InterVarsity Press, 1967), 77.

"I will cover your inadequacies and your flaws. I will cover your sins and clothe you in righteousness again. I will have to move heaven and earth to do it, and it will cost Me everything, including the life of My only Son. But I will get you back."

THE UNDOING OF JESUS

As Genesis 3:24 reveals, a way back into paradise does exist. God didn't completely seal off the entrance to the garden; He blocked it with a sword that turns every direction and is aflame with the fire of God. The only way for us to get back to the place where we trust the goodness of God again is if someone risks going through the sword to get us there. Believe it or not, someone made that sacrifice. The flaming sword of God fell on Jesus the day He hung on the cross. His amazing sacrifice—His ultimate and perfect covering—is what re-opened the entrance to paradise and enables us to commune with God once again.

At the cross, Jesus undid everything that went wrong in Genesis 3. In the garden of Eden, God told Adam, "Obey Me concerning this tree of the knowledge of good and evil, and you will live." Adam and Eve disobeyed. Yet in the garden of Gethsemane, God told Jesus, "Obey Me concerning this tree of crucifixion, and You will die." Jesus obeyed.

Adam and Eve took and ate of the forbidden tree. Their simple act of disobedience plunged them into a world they couldn't have imagined in their worst nightmare. They took and ate, and were immediately alienated from God. But in preparation for the cross, Jesus told His disciples, "Take and eat. This is My body that is broken for you. This is My blood that is shed for you." That meal symbolized Christ's ultimate act of obedience and made a way for God's children to once again commune with Him.

In Ezekiel 16, God metaphorically described who we are as a result of the fall and how He transforms us as a result of Christ's intervention. Apart from God, we're like a naked baby, abandoned in a field, still kicking in our own blood. Listen as these words are spoken over you from your Father:

> "As for your birth, your umbilical cord wasn't cut on the day you were born, and you weren't washed clean with water. You were not rubbed with salt or wrapped in cloths. No one cared enough about you to do even one of these things out of compassion for you. But you were thrown out into the open field because you were despised on the day you were born.
>
> "I passed by you and saw you lying in your blood, and I said to you as you lay in your blood: Live! Yes, I said to you as you lay in your blood: Live! I made you thrive like plants of the field. You grew up and matured and became

very beautiful. Your breasts were formed and your hair grew, but you were stark naked.

"Then I passed by you and saw you, and you were indeed at the age for love. So I spread the edge of My garment over you and covered your nakedness. I pledged Myself to you, I entered into a covenant with you, and you became Mine. This is the declaration of the Lord GOD. I washed you with water, rinsed off your blood, and anointed you with oil. I clothed you in embroidered cloth and provided you with leather sandals. I also wrapped you in fine linen and covered you with silk. I adorned you with jewelry, putting bracelets on your wrists and a chain around your neck. I put a ring in your nose, earrings on your ears, and a beautiful tiara on your head. So you were adorned with gold and silver, and your clothing was made of fine linen, silk, and embroidered cloth. You ate fine flour, honey, and oil. You became extremely beautiful and attained royalty" (Ezekiel 16:4-13).

Christian, you have no need for fig leaves. Through Jesus' substitutionary sacrifice, He made right the wrongs of the fall and restored everything that was lost in the garden of Eden. Know that God is good and you don't have to believe the serpent's promise that you'll find good in sin. You're fully known and loved, because at the cross, Jesus undid everything that went wrong. Despite the events of Genesis 3, God sees you and shouts, "Live!"

Think through the last few times you wrestled with obeying a certain command of God. Why did you wrestle?

What motivated your final obedience or disobedience? Was it your own wisdom or God's wisdom? Was your trust in yourself or in God?

Is God's Word and wisdom enough for you to choose obedience? If you disobey, what does that reveal about your trust in God?

Describe a specific time when you were deceived into thinking that God's withholding of something from you meant He was withholding everything from you.

Leading a group? It's the way to go. Find extra questions and teaching tools in the leader kit, available at *threadsmedia.com/creationunraveled.*

What are some of the dangers in thinking you know better than God what's good for your life? Would you say this is something you struggle with? Explain.

Identify specific areas of your life where God is commanding you to obey His Word. What "good" do you think God is withholding from you by telling you to obey? But in actuality, what "good" is He promising you if you obey Him?

Why is an offense against God so much greater than any other offense?

What are your fig leaves? What do you use to cover or hide yourself out of shame, fear, or guilt?

What does Jesus' sacrificial death on your behalf mean to you?

Have you ever thought about the fact that one of the repercussions of Jesus' death and resurrection is a restored Eden? What are the ramifications of this reality?

List the blessings from God that are mentioned in the Ezekiel 16 passage. What do they symbolize? What can we learn about God from that passage of Scripture?

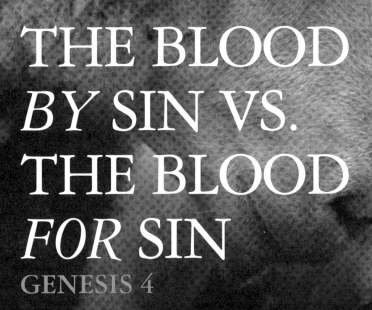

THE BLOOD
BY SIN VS.
THE BLOOD
FOR SIN

GENESIS 4

SESSION FOUR

"And while they were in the field, Cain attacked his brother Abel and killed him. Then the LORD said to Cain, 'Where is your brother Abel?' 'I don't know,' he replied. 'Am I my brother's guardian?' Then He said, 'What have you done? Your brother's blood cries out to Me from the ground!'"(Genesis 4:8-10).

As we continue through the Book of Genesis, we come to another story that teaches us more about sin. Sin can be a challenging topic to study, especially for an extended period of time. Learning more and more about the depths of our evil natures can feel like a broken record that begins breaking us. Inevitable questions plague our minds, such as, *Why does studying sin matter?* Or, *Why do I have to immerse myself in this when it feels so overwhelmingly defeating?* Or, *I get it; I'm a sinner. Can't we just move on?*

Sadly, you and I will never be able to fully grasp our sin because it runs deeper than our hearts would dare let us venture, for fear that we would be undone by what we found. We're not in danger of understanding our sin too much, of so grasping its darkness that it requires no additional attention. Our plight is quite the opposite. When we do the work of contemplating our sinful selves, we find that the horror of our sin is what leads us to the hope of a Savior. Without seeing the horror with our own eyes, we would never seek the hope. John Calvin addressed the importance of wrestling with sin in his book, *Institutes of the Christian Religion:*

> "Our wisdom, insofar as it ought to be deemed true and solid wisdom, consists almost entirely of two parts: the knowledge of God and of ourselves ... The miserable ruin into which the revolt of the first man has plunged us, compels us to turn our eyes upward ... We are accordingly urged by our own evil things to consider the good things of God; and, indeed, we cannot aspire to Him in earnest until we have begun to be displeased with ourselves. For what man is not disposed to rest in himself? Who, in fact, does not thus rest, so long as he is unknown to himself; that is, so long as he is contented with his own endowments, and unconscious or unmindful of his misery? Every person, therefore, on coming to the knowledge of himself, is not only urged to seek God, but is also led as by the hand to find him."[1]

The reason we must look at our sin so extensively now, even though we can't see the whole picture, is so we can treasure the solution to our problem all the more. Wrestling with sin won't help us feel better about ourselves, but that's OK because it's not supposed to. Instead of feeling better about ourselves, we'll feel better about God. The sweetness of our salvation will be magnified. The richness of God's mercy will be amplified.

A shallow, cursory diagnosis of a sickness doesn't lead to a cure; it leaves us with incomplete remedies that provide no hope of getting well. So it is with sin. In order to respond to sin in the vehement way Scripture commands, we have to realize how serious a threat sin is against us. Otherwise, we'll dismiss Scripture's warnings as too extreme, which is a mistake we can't afford to make.

1. John Calvin, *Institutes of the Christian Religion*, trans. Henry Beveridge, rev. ed. (Peabody, Massachusetts: Hendrickson Publishers, Inc., 2008), 4.

THE SECOND GENERATION

When we last read about Adam and Eve, they were cursed with consequences for their sins and cast out of the garden of Eden and the presence of God. Genesis 4 begins with Eve giving birth to two children:

> "Adam was intimate with his wife Eve, and she conceived and gave birth to Cain. She said, 'I have had a male child with the Lord's help.' Then she also gave birth to his brother Abel. Now Abel became a shepherd of flocks, but Cain worked the ground" (Genesis 4:1-2).

You may be familiar with what happened next in Cain and Abel's story. Both sons offered sacrifices to God from their respective areas of work—Cain gave produce, and Abel gave some of his flock—but God only accepted the sacrifice of Abel. When Cain realized that his offering was rejected, something started brewing in his heart, something dark and consuming (Genesis 4:4-5). The sin at root in Cain made itself known, and he was on the move to follow in the footsteps of his disobedient parents.

But before Cain got the chance to act on the evil desires brewing in his heart, God showed up and spoke truth into his life. Have you ever been in a situation like this? You stand on the brink of committing a sin, but the evil and righteousness within you are battling it out to see which you'll obey. You sense the conviction of the Holy Spirit, reminding you of God's truth, yet at the same time, you justify the sin you're about to commit. A war is raging within your soul. In that place of rebellion and evil is where God met Cain:

> "Then the Lord said to Cain, 'Why are you furious? And why do you look despondent? If you do what is right, won't you be accepted? But if you do not do what is right, sin is crouching at the door. Its desire is for you, but you must rule over it'" (Genesis 4:6-7).

God takes sin seriously, and He expects us to as well. He encouraged Cain to kill the sin within him before the sin killed him. Only one of them would come out alive. You may be surprised that God tried to discourage Cain from sinning, since sin had already tainted creation through Adam and Eve's rebellion. Because we tend to think of God as being like us, we might have expected Him to throw in the towel on humanity with an attitude like, "Oh well, sin ruined the perfect world and people I created. Who cares what Cain does?" Thankfully, God is nothing like us. Through the exchange with Cain, God revealed His holiness. He deeply cares about each and every act of sin in this world. He is neither cavalier nor dismissive. Every injustice will be accounted for, and none will go unpunished. The name of God that is tarnished with sin will be vindicated.

 Listen to "Come Ye Sinners" by the Robbie Seay Band from the *Creation Unraveled* playlist, available at *threadsmedia.com/creationunraveled.*

THE PROMISE OF SIN VS. THE PROMISE OF GOD

The problem Cain faced in Genesis 4:1-7 was that he didn't see things as they were; he saw them as he wanted them to be. This glimpse into his life from Genesis 4 reveals he weighed a heavy decision in his mind:

Option 1: Sin promises a certain reality. Through Cain's eyes, it could've seemed that Abel was a threat to him, because as long as Abel was around, God would never notice Cain. For Cain to be happy and have what he felt he deserved, Abel had to go.

Option 2: God promises a certain reality. Satan was crouched at the door, waiting to devour Cain. The very thing Cain contemplated doing to Abel, sin resolved to do to Cain. God showed His grace to Cain by warning him: "Fight, Cain! Resist this! You must see this evil for what it is, or it will kill you."[2]

These were the two juxtaposing "realities" Cain faced, but which one was real?

We know this scene all too well, don't we? We've seen the kindness of the Lord show up through His Spirit to fight for us and remind us of the battle we're in. He illuminates the danger we face, and we see sin crouching beside us, waiting to pounce. We pause and seek help from God through prayer and Scripture. We bring the temptation out into the open, so our brothers and sisters in Christ can fight alongside of us. We see things as they are, heed God's warning, and by the grace of God, act righteously.

Then there are the other times, when God reveals truth to us just before we trade everything for a lie. We ignore the gracious warnings of God and instead surrender to sin. We fall for the deception that this sin, whatever it may be, will be better for us than what God promises. The damage is always great, even if we try to convince ourselves otherwise. The warpath of sin in our lives leaves many casualties behind, but that isn't the entirety of its destruction. For days, months, and sometimes years following the act of sin, we're haunted by memories of our failure.

RESPONDING TO SIN

Our options for responding to temptation before we sin are straightforward—flee from the temptation or give in. But how do we respond to temptation *after* we've sinned? How do we face our countless failures? What do we do after we've traded God's counsel for the empty promises of sin? How do we prevent the guilt and shame of sin from destroying us and paralyzing us from seeking God?

Dr. John Piper addressed this issue when he spoke to one of the largest gatherings of college students in the nation at a Passion Conference in 2007. He shared his burden

---

 2. "Submit therefore to God. Resist the devil and he will flee from you. Draw near to God and He will draw near to you" (James 4:7-8).

for the tragic numbers of young people who dream radical dreams of living for Jesus, only to forsake those dreams because they feel disqualified by past sins. Their hearts used to say through tears, "Lord, I will lay everything down for You. No sacrifice is too great. My name does not matter. I want to spend my life making Your name famous among the nations!" But those same hearts have been marred with shame, reduced to apathetic morsels of what used to be the feasting table of their faith. Their dreams have been resigned to lesser things, such as middle-class security and comfort, because of the gnawing sense of unworthiness and guilt from countless sins.

The great tragedy here is that people can become so paralyzed by sin that they give up living the lives God called them to live. Dreams of living their faith with reckless abandon are replaced by the desire to fly under the radar, resigned to the sins that overtake them. All that's left of a once radical faith is the hope that God will have mercy on them in the end, because they certainly can't be used for the kingdom now. The sadness of this life is almost too much to bear when compared to what Christ purchased on the cross. Many of us were never taught how to deal with sin after it has been committed. We can't just be taught how not to fail, we also have to learn how to deal with failure in such a way that it doesn't discourage us from impacting God's kingdom. Piper explained it this way:

> "The tragedy is that Satan uses the guilt of [your] failures to strip you of every radical dream you ever had, or might have, and in its place give you a happy, safe, secure, American life of superficial pleasures until you die in your lake side rocking chair, wrinkled and useless, leaving a big fat inheritance to your middle-aged children to confirm them in their worldliness. That's the main tragedy."[3]

For the rest of this session, we'll focus on answering the question of how to fight sin after we've already sinned. God's response to Cain's sin and the events of Scripture that follow provide us hope for dealing with failure.

THE BLOOD SHED *BY* SIN

Let's read the rest of Cain's story.

> **"Cain said to his brother Abel, 'Let's go out to the field.' And while they were in the field, Cain attacked his brother Abel and killed him. Then the LORD said to Cain, 'Where is your brother Abel?' 'I don't know,' he replied. 'Am I my brother's guardian?' Then He said, 'What have you done? Your brother's blood cries out to Me from the ground!'" (Genesis 4:8-10).**

3. John Piper, "How to Deal with the Guilt of Sexual Failure for the Glory of Christ and His Global Cause" [cited 7 March 2011]. Available from the Internet: *desiringgod.org.*

Cain heard God's counsel to flee sin's temptation, but he didn't listen. His rage gave birth to sin, and when sin was accomplished in his heart, it brought forth death. The effect of sin is always death; it was for Cain and is for us. Cain committed the act he had contemplated, and the blood of his innocent brother was shed.

Evil continued its reign in the heart of humanity, which began with the first rebellion against God. In the midst of ongoing 'rejection, God again inserted Himself into His creation to fight for humanity and save us from ourselves. Still, we ignored God, belittling Him by declaring that we knew what was best for our lives. With Cain's act, the sin birthed from rage spilled innocent blood, and man's sin was multiplied.

Wasn't this the same lesson Cain heard his parents teach over and over again, using their mistake as the example of the wrong course of action to take? Why can't we understand that rejecting God always leads to death? This seems like the perfect opportunity for God to have grabbed Cain by the neck and shaken sense into him, which would've been a completely justified response. But that's not what God did.

God came to Cain. He sought him out and spoke with him. After Cain murdered his brother, God approached him in the same way He did before the sin occurred. By approaching him in this manner, God gave Cain ample opportunity to repent of his sin and beg for forgiveness for rejecting God and taking the life of his brother. God beckoned Cain, "Where is your brother? What have you done?" This is the heart of our God. Both before and after we sin, He seeks to save us from the evil that so desperately wants to consume us, showing Himself to be a gracious God indeed.

A GLIMPSE OF JUSTICE

Through His continued pursuit of Cain, God proved Himself gracious, but what about the fact that Abel was murdered? Didn't some kind of justice need to be poured out on Cain for his sin? You aren't the first person to wonder that. In Genesis 4:10, we read that the blood of Abel cried out to God. From the ground it was spilled on, the blood shed by sin cried out to God for the justice only He can deliver. And He must. God must deliver the justice the blood requires, or He isn't a just God.

We know God is just because it's one of His chief characteristics seen in Scripture (e.g. Isaiah 61:8; Micah 6:8; Luke 4:17-19). As a just God, He can't ignore injustice. If we were Abel, we certainly wouldn't want Him to ignore the injustice done to us. Our blood would cry out, too. When we've been offended, we see the need for justice so much more clearly than when we do the offending. God is a God of grace and mercy, without question, but He is also a God of justice. He must display both, and so He does:

"So now you are cursed, alienated, from the ground that opened its mouth to receive your brother's blood you have shed. If you work the ground, it will never again give you its yield. You will be a restless wanderer on the earth" (Genesis 4:11-12).

God enacted His righteous justice upon Cain when He cursed him for murdering his brother. God's curse penetrated to the core of Cain's identity. Up until that point, he was a farmer, a cultivator of the ground. But as a result of God's curse, he lost that identity. If Cain attempted to do what he had always done in the past, what he knew and excelled in, his efforts would be profitless. His purpose in life was gone.

We face the same threat as a consequence of our sin. God shows us limitless grace and mercy, but the unrepentant heart grows hardened and indifferent toward God over time. The things we were meant to do and find fulfillment in eventually cease to produce life-giving fruit.

COUNTERFEIT REPENTANCE

Not surprisingly, Cain had a response to God's deliverance of justice:

"But Cain answered the LORD, 'My punishment is too great to bear! Since You are banishing me today from the soil, and I must hide myself from Your presence and become a restless wanderer on the earth, whoever finds me will kill me'" (Genesis 4:13-14).

Cain was clearly sorrowful before the Lord. One can sense great despair in his response, and his cry to God was likely through sobs of grief and pain. He seemed to be repenting. He was sorry, after all. But did Cain demonstrate biblical repentance, or perhaps something else?

Augustine described sin as man being "turned toward himself."[4] His point is that sin always focuses on the self. It elevates self above everything and everyone, including God and others. God's created beings shift their concentration from Him, their Creator, and redirect it to themselves. Sin is not merely doing bad things; it's far more complex than that. It's so ingrained in us that even when we try to do "good" things, like giving to the poor, entering into relationships with others, attending church, or studying the Bible, the human heart can turn them into ways we can serve ourselves and our own interests rather than God and others.

For example, we may give to the poor and then somehow believe God owes us since we did something for Him. Or we may study Scripture, but only so that we can look

---

4. Saint Augustine, *City of God*, trans. Gerald G. Walsh, Demetrius B. Zema, Grace Monahan, and Daniel J. Honan, ed. Vernon J. Bourke (New York: Doubleday, 1958), 309.

smart and "godly" in front of others. Many of us do good not because we truly love God and want to obey Him, but because deep down inside, we believe it makes us look good or gives us leverage with God.

The danger is that we can be so focused on ourselves that even when we repent we do so with false motivations, whether we know it or not. In Psalm 78, we see an example of repentance from the Israelites, who were being disciplined by God for living in disobedience to Him. Look at how their repentance was tainted:

> **"When He killed some of them, the rest began to seek Him; they repented and searched for God. They remembered that God was their rock, the Most High God, their Redeemer. But they deceived Him with their mouths, they lied to Him with their tongues, their hearts were insincere toward Him, and they were unfaithful to His covenant" (Psalm 78:34-37).**

Their repentance was tainted by flattery, lying, and unfaithfulness. It was a counterfeit repentance.

Cain was sorrowful. We saw his anguish and pain. But what was the root of his mourning?

> **"My punishment is too great to bear!" (Genesis 4:13).**

Therein lies Cain's tragedy. This is a man who sinned by taking the life of his brother, a child of God, but we don't hear him crying out about that. He wasn't concerned about the cost his sin had on God's honor and glory. He wasn't moved to tears over his brother lying innocently in his own blood. Instead, he cried out to God with the attitude, "I'm sorry! I can't handle what's going to happen to me. This is too much for me to bear." Cain's repentance was motivated by the consequences God threatened, not by the grievous sin he committed. How tragic that Cain's repentance was just as self-absorbed and self-centered as the sin that preceded it.

We can easily see an attitude like Cain's and become indignant. "How could Cain be so selfish? All he cares about is himself and what's going to happen to him. I'm so thankful that I'm not like him!" It's infuriating to us, isn't it? Yes, until we step back and see that we're just like Cain.

Our responses to sin often mirror Cain's. Sure, sometimes we can honestly say we're truly sorry for the sin, not its consequences. We may even shed tears for the way we've dishonored God and seek repentance for that. Maybe that is true for some of us after we sin.

 Watch the *Creation Unraveled* video "The Blood *by* Sin vs. the Blood *for* Sin," available at *threadsmedia. com/creationunraveled.*

Or maybe that's what we want to be true.

Counterfeit repentance has a striking resemblance to the real thing, especially at first glance. The results of both are usually tears, anguish, regret, and the promise to never repeat the sin again. Not until we look beneath the surface, into the depths of our hearts, do we see the stark contrast between counterfeit and genuine repentance. Counterfeit repentance is always chiefly concerned with the effects to the self. The turn toward self can be so subtle and natural that it's unrecognizable at times. When we're falsely repentant, we don't make apologies for the muddying of God's name, nor do we shed tears over the damage done to others. We're only apologetic for the pain brought upon ourselves. We weep only for our own losses.

A GLIMPSE OF MERCY

The selfish motivation for repentance modeled by Cain reveals the level of deception we're under when we're mastered by sin. Consider this: The God of the universe is offended when we sin. He is the living, true God; we have no higher authority to which we may appeal. He is eternal and holds all things—the mountains, oceans, and cells within our bodies—in place by the power of His word. He knit together every fiber of being within every person in all of the earth. Our God has the power to bring both physical and spiritual death upon us and banish our souls to hell for eternity, and in doing so remain completely just and holy. As the psalmist so eloquently put it:

> "Before the mountains were born, before You gave birth to the earth and the world, from eternity to eternity, You are God. You return mankind to the dust, saying, 'Return, descendants of Adam.' For in Your sight a thousand years are like yesterday that passes by, like a few hours of the night. You end their lives; they sleep. They are like grass that grows in the morning—in the morning it sprouts and grows; by evening it withers and dries up" (Psalm 90:2-6).

This is the God who is offended when we sin.

Yet who do we turn to in repentance? How do we mourn? We weep at the altar of ourselves, often neglecting God altogether. Do you see the insanity in this? This is like murdering someone in cold blood, and then crying because their innocent blood soiled your clothes. Or like cheating on your spouse and being mad because he or she won't forgive you. Counterfeit repentance exposes our depraved hearts more than the initial sin did. This is the heart that most of us, like Cain, have beating inside our chests. If not for the grace of God to keep our affections on Him, this kind of repentance can distract us from reality as easily as it did Cain in this Old Testament story.

Isn't it amazing to think that our tears need washing? Can you believe that even our repentance sometimes needs to be repented of? And yet, God's mercy isn't dependent upon our abilities, even our ability to correctly repent. Just as God demonstrated His justice by cursing Cain because of the blood that was shed, at the same time He displayed how merciful He is. When we are faithless, even in our repentance, God still remains faithful. Read God's response to Cain's "repentance":

> "Then the Lord replied to him, 'In that case, whoever kills Cain will suffer vengeance seven times over.' And He placed a mark on Cain so that whoever found him would not kill him. Then Cain went out from the Lord's presence and lived in the land of Nod, east of Eden" (Genesis 4:15-16).

As God banished Cain from his homeland, Cain cried out in fear that others would try to avenge Abel's death by taking his life. Not surprisingly, Cain appeared unmoved by the fact that God spared his life, further evidence that Cain's fear and shame were misplaced. God's righteous anger had many opportunities to be kindled throughout this story. For the second time, Cain rejected God by fearing humanity more. Still, God's mercy is magnified in His promise to protect Cain's life.

God assured Cain that the very sin he committed against his brother would be punished seven-fold if someone attempted to do the same to Cain. What mercy of God! Scripture doesn't specify what the "sign for Cain" was, but this wasn't the first time God put a mark of protection on His child. As God banished Cain's parents from the garden of Eden, He first sacrificed an animal to make them protective clothes. Both the clothing provided for Adam and Eve and the mark given to Cain foreshadowed something to come. These markers pointed to God's ultimate display of mercy in the lives of His people—the shed blood of Jesus for the redemption of our souls. From the beginning of Genesis, God points us to our need for His perfect and righteous justice for our sin of rebellion against Him. To Cain, God handed down a punishment that seemed unbearable. At the same time, however, God covered His unrepentant child, who repeatedly rejected Him, with a blanket of mercy. God doesn't choose to be either merciful or just; He's always both.

SNAPSHOTS OF GOD'S GLORY

While it's encouraging to see God's justice and mercy displayed through the story of Cain and Abel, something is lacking. I (Halim) get the impression that God isn't displaying either aspect of His character fully. He seems to be holding back, not completely offering Himself to man. We know from other instances in Scripture that God's restraint is good news for Cain. If God had revealed Himself fully, Cain wouldn't have lived through the moment. For example, toward the end of Moses' life, he asked to see God in the fullness of His glory:

 "Here is individual responsibility and the invention of conscience. You can if you will but it is up to you. This little story turns out to be one of the most profound in the world. I always felt it was but now I know it is." —John Steinbeck, author of *East of Eden*, on the story of Cain and Abel.[i]

"Then Moses said, 'Please, let me see Your glory.' He said, 'I will cause all My goodness to pass in front of you, and I will proclaim the name Yahweh before you. I will be gracious to whom I will be gracious, and I will have compassion on whom I will have compassion.' But He answered, 'You cannot see My face, for no one can see Me and live.' The LORD said, 'Here is a place near Me. You are to stand on the rock, and when My glory passes by, I will put you in the crevice of the rock and cover you with My hand until I have passed by. Then I will take My hand away, and you will see My back, but My face will not be seen'" (Exodus 33:18-23).

Moses begged God, "Show me Your glory. I want to see You!" If God intended to show His face to anyone, you would think it would've been Moses. Moses is the one God spoke to through the burning bush, the one God called to lead His people out of Egypt, the one for whom God parted the sea. To say Moses was intimate with God is an understatement. But even he couldn't look on the fullness of God and live. God told Moses that without holding back some of Himself, Moses would surely die. So, God hid Moses in the cleft of a rock and covered him with His hand as He passed by. Can you imagine what it would be like to be hidden beneath the hand of God as He allowed you to get a glimpse of how glorious He truly is?

In the story of Cain and Abel, and all throughout the stories of the Old Testament, we get small glimpses of God, snapshots of His justice, righteousness, mercy, grace, and love. If God showed Cain the fullness of His justice for the injustice of shedding his brother's blood, then Cain would've been killed immediately and sent to hell for an eternity of punishment. In this situation, God's mercy would have to be expensed for the sake of His full display of justice.

Consider also the reverse. If God showed the fullness of His mercy to Cain in those moments following his sin, he would've been instantaneously forgiven for Abel's murder. God would've said, "Cain, I forgive you all your transgressions. I love you and am for you in every way. I am going to take you up into My kingdom now and you will dwell there forever with Me." God would be profoundly and fully merciful in that moment, but would He also be able to demonstrate His justice? No, His justice would need to be expensed for the sake of His full display of mercy.

Are you noticing the problem here? How can God display the fullness of His justice without humanity being consumed and destroyed forever? And how can God display the fullness of His mercy without compromising His justice? Will we ever be able to see God without Him holding back for our sake?

THE BLOOD SHED *FOR* SIN

At one point in history, the complete measure of God's justice intersected with the full portrait of His mercy for us to see—at the cross of Jesus Christ. Here we don't focus on the blood that was shed *by* sin, but instead we see the perfect blood that was shed *for* sin. The cross is the way God chose to offer Himself fully to us.[5]

If, because of our sin, God condemned us to hell forever, would He be just? Absolutely. Would He be merciful? No. He wouldn't have the opportunity to be merciful to us because we would always be serving our due penalty in hell, the result of His justice. And if, even though we sinned against God, He completely and fully forgave us, if He swept every dirty deed and awful action under the rug and erased our debt completely, would He be merciful? No doubt about it. But would He be just? He couldn't be. Nice, yes. But just? No.

At the wonderful cross, we witness the impossible. God fully demonstrated His justice. Holding nothing back, He poured out His full wrath against sin. At the same time, God fully demonstrated His mercy. Instead of pouring out His wrath on us, the rebellious people who fully deserved it, He poured it out on His perfect, holy Son. The guilty were spared at the expense of God Himself.

At the cross, the blood shed *for* sin answered the cry of the blood shed *by* sin. The writer of Hebrews said it best:

> **"For you have not come to what could be touched, to a blazing fire, to darkness, gloom, and storm, to the blast of a trumpet, and the sound of words. (Those who heard it begged that not another word be spoken to them, for they could not bear what was commanded: And if even an animal touches the mountain, it must be stoned! The appearance was so terrifying that Moses said, I am terrified and trembling.) Instead, you have come to Mount Zion, to the city of the living God (the heavenly Jerusalem), to myriads of angels in festive gathering, to the assembly of the firstborn whose names have been written in heaven, to God who is the Judge of all, to the spirits of righteous people made perfect, to Jesus (mediator of a new covenant), and to the sprinkled blood, which says better things than the blood of Abel"** (Hebrews 12:18-24).

In his sermon titled "What were we put in the world to do?," Tim Keller further expands on the connection between Christ's work on the cross and the Cain and Abel story. He explains that the blood of Jesus—the blood shed *for* sin—solves the problem of "the justice-mercy tension." Keller states:

---

 5. *"For God was pleased to have all His fullness dwell in Him, and through Him to reconcile everything to Himself by making peace through the blood of His cross—whether things on earth or things in heaven" (Colossians 1:19-20).*

"How can God continue to offer mercy and hope to the Cains of the world who have slain the Abels of the world? The Hebrews author in this brilliant metaphor puts it like this: 'The ultimate Abel, the ultimate man of faith, the only true and literally innocent man came into the world and we—Cains all—killed him. But this was not a random accident. This one came into the world to be our substitute, to bear the curse that we Cains deserved.'"[6]

Jesus took on the curse of Cain. Cain became a restless wanderer (Genesis 4:14), and likewise, Jesus told His disciples, "Foxes have holes and the birds of the air have their nests, but the Son of man has nowhere to lay His head." Jesus was tracked down in the garden of Gethsemane, and later He was killed. And Jesus felt temporarily abandoned from God as He hung on the cross and cried, "My God, My God, why have You forsaken Me?" Jesus became the curse on our behalf, on behalf of all the Cains of the world.

Abel's blood screamed out to God. The blood shed *by* sin demanded justice. Through angst and pain, the blood shed *by* sin made its case to be vindicated. The blood of Jesus, the blood shed *for* sin, would satisfy that cry for justice and vindication. All of God's wrath against the sins of His people were satisfied in the blood of Jesus. Justice was served, and as a result we're all free from the guilt that was ours to bear. It is finished.

Even My Failure?
If you're a believer in Christ, if the blood that was shed for sin covers you, then every sin you have committed and will commit has been dealt with justly. Every sinful emotion, thought, attitude, and action has been duly punished and the payment has been received in full. Every drop of God's wrath that was stored up for your sins was poured out onto Christ. Every single drop.

While in theory we may accept the idea that God took on our sins, reminding ourselves of this truth in the midst of those sins that plague us can be challenging. Surely God didn't mean that He would keep showing us mercy for the same sins over and over again, did He? We know He took everything on at the cross, but when we're in the grips of habitual, repetitive sin, it's hard to imagine His mercy persevering. We want to appeal to His mercy, but we can't help but wonder if He'll grow tired of giving it to us.

Back when I was just starting college, I really tried for the first time in my life to obey Scripture. I believed that what God said was best for my life would actually be better than anything I could come up with. Like everyone else, I wasn't perfect. I longed to be radically obedient to Christ, but I still saw sin in my life. When I responded to this sin, I would go to God and ask Him to forgive me. Each time I approached Him, though, a sense of nervousness came over me. I begged Him saying, "God, will You be merciful

6. Dr. Timothy J. Keller, *What were we put in the world to Do?* (New York: Redeemer Presbyterian Church, 2006), 62.

to me? Will You be gracious to me and forgive me?" And then a few days later, I'd sin in the same way again, and again I'd beg for mercy. I hated this cycle. I grew more and more nervous that I was kindling up His anger. "This time will be different. I promise I will never let this happen again," I would assure God.

Does this conversation sound familiar to you? I now realize that although deep in the trenches of my heart I believed God was merciful, I had this notion that His mercy had a threshold and I must be getting dangerously close to it. Surely God would forgive a young man in his late teenage years who was trying to get his life together. But what if the same struggle was still in my life next year? Or in 10 years? Or when I'm in my 50s? How could I expect God to continue to show me mercy then? At what point would He run out of patience with me? In these moments, I was overwhelmed with shame, guilt, and fear that my habitual sin would be my ruin. I viewed my struggle with sin as the marker on me that my life was resigned to be ineffective and fruitless forever. How could I trust God to use me when I couldn't even get my life together?

In moments like these, Cain's story brings the most comfort. All of God's wrath was fully poured out on Jesus when He went to the cross. Our sins have been justly paid for, which means nothing else is owed. Debt doesn't loom over the heads of God's children; nothing is left for us to do but worship this great God who stands in our place. God is merciful to forgive us, yes, but He is also just and righteous in His forgiveness. He can't require more from us than has already been paid. And, Christian, He would never require more.

God was infinitely offended by our rebellion against Him. The debt we owed Him was great, more than we could ever imagine and more than we could ever pay. The great news for us is that the depths of His satisfaction in His Son's sacrifice far exceeded the depths of our offense. God is more pleased and satisfied by the atonement of Jesus than He was angered by our cosmic rejection (cf. Romans 8; Hebrews 2:5-18). That speaks to the value of Jesus' act, not to the smallness of our sin. As we gaze at the cross, we're not only confronted with overwhelming evidence for God's mercy, but we're also given holy assurance that God's justice has been satisfied and He'll never again punish us for the sins that plague us.

For some, this concept is so foreign that it sounds heretical. Is this anywhere in the Bible? I'm glad you asked:

> **"But if we walk in the light as He Himself is in the light, we have fellowship with one another, and the blood of Jesus His Son cleanses us from all sin. If we say, 'We have no sin,' we are deceiving ourselves, and the truth is**

Listen to "Healing Is in Your Hands" by Christy Nockels from the *Creation Unraveled* playlist, available at *threadsmedia.com/creationunraveled*.

not in us. If we confess our sins, He is faithful and righteous to forgive us our sins and to cleanse us from all unrighteousness" (1 John 1:7-9).

John doesn't say that if we confess our sins, God will be faithful and *merciful* to forgive our sins. Nor does he say that God will be faithful and *loving*. The Word of God assures us that in the moments when God is forgiving sins, He is being faithful and *just*.

Our Great Advocate

In the courtroom of our lives, God is both the Judge and the infinitely wronged Defendant. We sit on trial in the middle of the room, deafened by people shouting out our many failures and causing us to relive every horrible, shameful act we've done. Satan leads the charge to seal our feeling of guilt. When we're on the brink of succumbing to every taunt, the room goes silent. The one Person in the room who has every right to condemn and sentence us—the Defendant—does something else entirely. He intervenes on our behalf. He points to the blood spilling from His hands and feet and declares us innocent because He served our sentence.

Jesus is our Advocate when we sin. He says back to the Father, "Yes, Your character demands justice for these sins. You must collect the wage of sin, which is death; but I've done it. I paid for them with My blood, the blood that was shed for their sins. Your justice also demands that You never condemn those who I died for. You can't take two payments for the same sin."

The Justice to Forgive

Herein lies our answer to the question we posed at the beginning of this session: How do we fight sin after we've already sinned? Understanding Jesus as our Advocate changes everything for us as we struggle through our sins. We don't have to timidly approach the throne of God and ask Him over and over again to be merciful and gracious. Of course we need God's mercy and grace, but because of the blood of Jesus, we already have both. Instead, we can boldly approach God's throne and ask Him to demonstrate His great justice by cleansing us from all unrighteousness. God doesn't just tenderly forgive us because He is merciful; He ferociously forgives us because He is just.

Finally, we can deal with our guilt, the feelings that have plagued us for much longer than the sins themselves. Overcoming guilt is such a defeating challenge because we have only seen God as merciful. We see that mercy displayed and cling to it, and we thank God for the mercy He showed us in sending His Son to die on our behalf. But we must expand our view of the cross to include God's beautiful, comforting justice. His mercy demands that He forgive us, but His justice demands it as well. And because both were present at the cross, we're covered in Christ's righteousness, which leaves no room for guilt or shame.

The truths we hold onto for greatest comfort are made possible because of this promise of God's justice. We can lift our hands and sing, "Therefore, no condemnation now exists for those in Christ Jesus" (Romans 8:1). We can celebrate with the proclamation, "Who can bring an accusation against God's elect? God is the One who justifies" (Romans 8:33). We can be confident that nothing separates us from the love of God in Christ Jesus. We are secured. We are covered by the blood that was shed for sin.

Christian, you can dream that radical dream of paradise once again.

THE DANGER OF DELIBERATE SIN

Before we move on from Genesis 4, let me offer a word of caution for any who hear this sweet truth and feel as though they have a license to go on sinning because the blood of Jesus has been shed for them. Beware. To trample God's great grace and continue rejecting His provision is the distinguishing mark of an unbeliever. Paul tells us in Romans that the condemnation of such people is just (Romans 3:8), and the writer of Hebrews warns:

> "For if we deliberately sin after receiving the knowledge of the truth, there no longer remains a sacrifice for sins, but a terrifying expectation of judgment and the fury of a fire about to consume the adversaries . . . How much worse punishment do you think one will deserve who has trampled on the Son of God, regarded as profane the blood of the covenant by which he was sanctified, and insulted the Spirit of grace?" (Hebrews 10:26-27,29).

It is a terrifying thing to fall into the hands of the living God and not be covered by the blood of Jesus. If you only see His precious blood as a license to sin, be assured that you do not have saving faith in our most patient Father. Fall on your face and beg Him to change your heart to cherish His grace, not trample upon it.

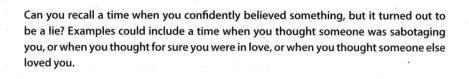

Can you recall a time when you confidently believed something, but it turned out to be a lie? Examples could include a time when you thought someone was sabotaging you, or when you thought for sure you were in love, or when you thought someone else loved you.

Share an example of a situation in your life that testifies to our ability to believe what we want to believe, rather than what is true.

Contrary to how you might read Genesis 4, God didn't approach Cain out of wrath, He approached Him out of grace and love. Can you recount a time in your life when you messed up so badly that you expected a punishment from God that you couldn't possibly bear?

Many times God disciplines us as a loving Father, but even more often, He graciously offers us counsel and a gentle opportunity to repent. Share about a time when God didn't deal with your sin as it deserved to be dealt with.

Leading a group? It's the way to go. Find extra questions and teaching tools in the leader kit, available at *threadsmedia.com/creationunraveled.*

Make a chart that lists the sins you struggle with and the ways you've attempted to repent from them. Examine each sin and your repentance, and try to answer honestly if your repentance was genuine or counterfeit. What were you truly sorry about in each situation—the cost to God's glory or the cost to yourself?

How does recognizing that Christ satisfied the wrath you deserve from God change your view of the cross?

What things have caused you to carry shame and guilt around for years?

What are some of the dreams you had of living for Christ that you've sacrificed because of this shame and guilt?

The gospel shows us that God is not only merciful, but He is just in forgiving us of our sin. How and why should this truth set you free from the shame and guilt of sin? In what ways does it free you up to dream radically for Jesus once again?

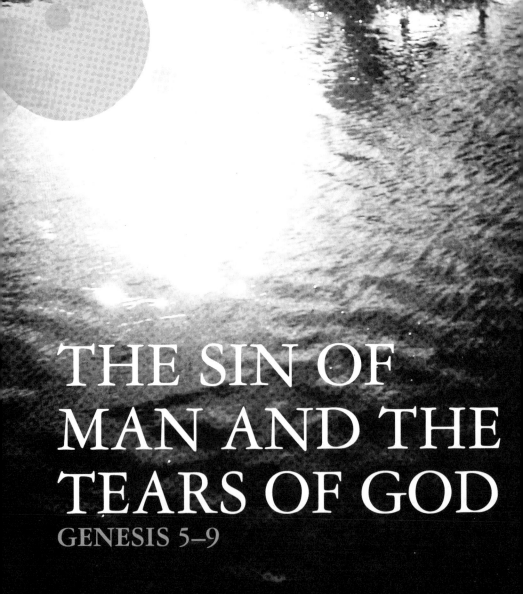

THE SIN OF MAN AND THE TEARS OF GOD

GENESIS 5–9

SESSION FIVE

"In the six hundredth year of Noah's life, in the second month, on the seventeenth day of the month, on that day all the sources of the watery depths burst open, the floodgates of the sky were opened, and the rain fell on the earth 40 days and 40 nights" (Genesis 7:11-12).

Genesis 5 brings us to one of the most referenced and illustrated stories of the Old Testament—Noah's ark. The story of Noah's ark is famous for its cute animals and the multi color rainbow that aids children in learning their colors. But as we look beyond the familiarity of this story, you may start to wonder why such images are popular for nurseries and baby clothes.

Don't get me (Halim) wrong, I've fallen for the marketing spin to this story myself. Who doesn't love a kid who can sing the whole Noah's arky-arky song? However, we'd be remiss if we didn't take a closer look at the biblical text. It won't take long for you to see that there's much more to this story than lovable animals and pretty rainbows. We're getting a little ahead of ourselves, though. First, let's refresh our memories of what happened in the first four chapters of Genesis.[i]

RECAP

"In the beginning God created the heavens and the earth" (Genesis 1:1).

Now, wait a second. Did that sink in? Or have you heard that profound statement so many times that it has lost its wonder? I know I lose sight of the grandeur of things when they're no longer new. The opening line of Genesis describes a rather significant event—the creation of the universe by God. What we read in Genesis is part of the amazing story God wrote to teach us about Himself. Allow that to sink in so you can connect with familiar Scripture passages in a fresh way.

God spoke the heavens and the earth into existence through the power of His word. He separated the light from the darkness, laid the foundation of the ocean and restricted its tide, and even taught the birds how to fly. He numbered the stars and created the wind. After it all, God made the pinnacle of His creation, the creature everything else was made to serve—a human.

"So God created man in His own image; He created him in the image of God; He created them male and female" (Genesis 1:27).

God brought this special part of creation into being a little differently than everything else. He formed humanity with His own hands, rather than His words, and intimately breathed life into his nostrils. Then the God of the universe gave humanity something no other fiber of creation had, nor would ever have—His image. God's image gave us an exclusive level of dignity that's ours for the rest of time.

However, following the good news of creation, we read in Genesis 3 about the greatest loss mankind has suffered. Adam and Eve failed to trust in the goodness of God, despite

Listen to "Joy Is in Our Hearts" by Sara Groves from the *Creation Unraveled* playlist, available at *threadsmedia.com/creationunraveled*.

His provisions, and sin ravaged the hearts of them both. Had Adam and Eve's mistake been as far as sin's damage reached, we might not think the fall was so significant. But as chapter 4 illustrated, sin wasn't isolated to the natures of Adam and Eve. It spread like an epidemic, infecting every human heart to follow.

THE SCOPE OF SIN

The only quality of sin more horrific than its 100 percent infection rate is the way its strength penetrates further and further into the human heart as it travels through the human race. The effects of sin seem to multiply before our very eyes throughout the stories of Genesis. Adam's shame turned into Cain's indifference, as evidenced by his response to God's inquiry about Abel: "Am I my brother's guardian?" (Genesis 4:9). Later in Genesis 4, we see the entitlement Lamech, a descendent of Cain, felt to sin as he cited God's protection of Cain as immunity for murder:

> "Lamech said to his wives: Adah and Zillah, hear my voice; wives of Lamech, pay attention to my words. For I killed a man for wounding me, a young man for striking me. If Cain is to be avenged seven times over, then for Lamech it will be seventy-seven times!" (Genesis 4:23-24).

From there sin spread into the descendents of Seth (known as the sons of God) as they took the daughters of men (descendents of Cain) for their wives (Genesis 6:1-4).[1] Without question, sin was the most severe problem facing humanity, and God was the most aware of this disease:

> "When the LORD saw that man's wickedness was widespread on the earth and that every scheme his mind thought of was nothing but evil all the time" (Genesis 6:5).

With every outward action of people's hands and through every inward thought of their hearts they said, "God, we don't trust You. We don't believe You." What a terrifying concept. This was true in humanity's early days and is just as true today for everyone who hasn't been given a new, regenerated heart.

When we reach this point in Genesis 6, humanity had become so infiltrated with sin that only one true believer remained on all of the earth. His name was Noah. Think about how profound that statement is. God looked down upon the earth and saw only one person who believed Him. Today the world contains approximately 6.9 billion people.[2] Can you imagine if only one person out of 6.9 billion believed in God? I can only imagine the treacheries and horrors that would surround him or her. What a daunting thought.

---

 1. *Nephilim* (Genesis 6:4) literally means "fallen ones," but it is unclear who this group of people was. Based on the mention of them in Numbers 13:33, many people conclude they were a race of giants.

2. *http://www.census.gov*

Some scientists estimate that the world's population in Noah's day, prior to the flood, was much larger than it is today—as many as 17 billion people.[3] If that number is accurate, Noah was the only person out of 16 billion, 999 million, 999 thousand and 999 who worshiped and trusted God. Everyone else hated God, or worse, ignored Him altogether.

This is the world God saw when He looked down from His heavenly throne. His creation had come a long way from the garden of Eden. But God's response to our rebellion may surprise you. Scripture doesn't say God was angry with the wickedness of His children, although that's the emotion we probably expect. Add this to the list of what's different between God and us. According to Genesis 6:6, the emotion God felt was grief:

> "... the Lord regretted that He had made man on the earth, and He was grieved in His heart."

God looked at His rebellious children and felt grief. Anguish. Sorrow.

If that doesn't give you a clear picture of the compassionate heart of our God, I don't know what will. Our sins cause God anguish. Consider the weight of that statement. As the psalmist said:

> "What is man that You remember him, the son of man that You look after him?" (Psalm 8:4).

Who are we that God would grieve over us? Does His grieving mean we're so significant that He *should* grieve over us? That seems unlikely. A closer look at the Hebrew word translated "grief" in Genesis 6:6 gives us a clue as to why it's God's emotional response to our sin.

In the Hebrew language, the word used for grief, *nakham*, translates as "a deep, unfulfilled longing; deep pain and bitter anguish." This seems like a strange word to describe a feeling the Creator experiences. God's grieving heart reveals something very unique about His character. He voluntarily—and that's an important distinction—bound His heart and life up with ours.[4] Obviously He didn't have to do that. God doesn't need us. But in creating us, He knit His heart to ours. The purest of hearts joined together with the vilest of hearts, voluntarily. This connection is so intimate that when the almighty Creator sees something go terribly wrong in our lives, He experiences deep, unimaginable pain.

The story of the flood details an intense time of suffering for humanity. At first glance, that suffering and one family's survival seems to be the centerpiece of the story. But Genesis 6:6 reveals that the backdrop of all human suffering is a God who suffers infinitely more.

---

3. *http://www.answersingenesis.org*

4. Tim Keller, "Lord of the Storm," preached on 3 December 2000 [cited 7 March 2011]. Available from the Internet: *redeemer.com*.

SESSION FIVE CREATION UNRAVELED

THE TEARS OF GOD

In his book, *Lament for a Son*, former Yale University professor of philosophy Nicholas Wolterstorff wrote, "The tears of God are the meaning of history."[5] What does he mean by such a claim? How do the tears of God have anything to do with history?

According to Genesis 3:7, the first humans essentially told God He wasn't worthy of their obedience because He isn't good and can't be trusted. And just like that, they turned away from Him. So why is there a Genesis 3:8? Why didn't God end history right then and there, instead of enduring with us?

Beyond that, we see in Genesis 6:5 that the people's rebellion worsened and every intention of their hearts was all evil, all the time. Could it get any worse? Surely not. If ever God was going to pull the plug, that was the time. But again God endured with us, and we have a Genesis 6:6. Why did He continue to endure with us? Why all the effort to build an ark, round up the animals, and save Noah and his family so humanity would survive? Why are we still here?

In Genesis 6:6 we see God suffering, voluntarily, for the sins of the world. That's why we're here—because God chose to weep. His heart grieved over what His children did, how they were wasting away under the power of sin and signing their souls over to darkness for eternity. The only reason we have any history at all is because He chose to suffer.

A KNOWING GRIEF

The fact that God bound His heart with ours and graciously allowed humanity to live is both surprising and comforting. We wouldn't be here if He hadn't! When we see this type of character on display, our patient and enduring God is almost more than we can handle. But that's not all.

Not only does our God grieve over us as we rebel against Him, our rebellion doesn't surprise Him. He knew we would sin before He made us, and He wasn't shocked by our rejection of Him. Instead, He decided to endure with us because He's gracious and loving. The reality is that God, knowing all the ways we would rebel and belittle Him, still knit us together with Himself. As a Father and a Creator, He breathed life into our nostrils. And in that moment of creation, He fully knew all the grief we would later cause Him. God joyfully and lovingly created you with His own hands, even though He knew all the ways your sin would hurt Him.

God knew that in order for history to continue and for His children to live, He had to suffer more than anyone could ever imagine. Our lives would cost Him greatly, but He knowingly chose to grieve.

5. Nicholas Wolterstorff, *Lament for a Son* (Grand Rapids, Michigan: Wm. B. Eerdmans Publishing, 1987) 90.

A WILLING GRIEF

Have you ever willingly chosen to do something that would cause you great pain because you knew the pain would be worth it in the end? If you're a parent, then you have, and you can understand why God let humanity continue to live.

Whether you're a parent or not, you know that raising children isn't an effortless process with no crises or rough patches. We faced numerous trials when we were growing up, and our children will too. Children disobey their parents and let them down. We did many things that caused our parents pain, and our children will also cause us pain. If you think you can have children who won't cause you grief, you're in for a big surprise!

The tricky thing about having a child is that a little person is by your side all the time. And that child wields the power to hurt you in ways you never imagined. Children can cause pain in parts of your heart that you didn't even know existed.

When my son Malachi was 2-and-a-half years old, we visited old friends in Fort Worth, Texas, and ate at one of our favorite restaurants. After spending quite a while in the restaurant, eating and chatting, we decided to take our conversation outside and free up our table. The restaurant had lots of seating outside and the weather was nice. One large, red metal bench caught Malachi's eye as soon as he saw it, but I noticed it had several sharp edges. I repeatedly told him not to climb on it, but of course he disobeyed.

As my wife and I continued our conversation with our friends, we were interrupted by what sounded like a hammer coming down on a nail followed by a horrific screeching cry. Malachi had tried to climb up the bench, slipped backwards, and slammed the back of his head into a sharp piece of metal. I ran to him as fast as I could and held him.

As I was holding him, I felt something warm dripping down my arm and realized that Malachi was gushing blood from the back of his head. All I could think about was getting him to the hospital so he could get the help he needed. I know I'm not the only parent who's had an experience like this—it's almost a parenting guarantee that you'll end up in the emergency room at some point.

In the moments of Malachi's pain, I was grieved; deeply grieved. The pain I felt in my heart was so intense I nearly doubled over from it. As my wife and I were sitting in the emergency room, an unnerving thought entered my mind: This would be the first of many trips to the hospital for us.

I knew that this torture in my heart wouldn't be an isolated event. Malachi would cause us this unimaginable pain again and again. At the same time that realization came to

---

 Watch the *Creation Unraveled* video "The Sin of Man and the Tears of God," available at *threadsmedia. com/creationunraveled.*

mind, another thought soon followed: I'd have this accident-prone, grief-causing child all over again. I knew that wasn't the only time he'd cause me pain and grief, but the pain was worth it.

Why? Why in the world would I willingly allow myself to suffer this kind of agony? Why would I have this kid all over again, knowing how much he makes my heart hurt? Because he's mine.

Isaiah painted the same portrait of our relationship with God:

> **"Can a woman forget her nursing child, or lack compassion for the child of her womb? Even if these forget, yet I will not forget you"** (Isaiah 49:15).

God's compassion for us is greater than a mother's compassion on her newborn child. He's crazy about us. He knew we would cause Him grief, but He gave us life anyway, and He would do it all over again. He's willing to suffer so that we may live. God showed us just how much He'll endure for our sake when He sacrificed His own Son for us. Every Old Testament story about people's sins points to the cross, the climactic example of God's willingness to grieve.[6] The story told in Genesis 6–9 includes three components that explicitly point to Jesus and the gospel—Noah, the flood, and the rainbow. Let's see what we can learn from each aspect of this story.

NOAH—A RIGHTEOUS MAN

Noah was the only believer in a world that had turned its back on God, and God extended him an offer of salvation:

> **"Noah, however, found favor in the sight of the Lord"** (Genesis 6:8).

God saw something in Noah that pleased Him. Wiping out everyone and bringing an end to our story was never God's plan. He intended to redeem an undeserving people so they would endure, as He had done many times already. A remnant would survive the tragedy of the flood, and Noah, a "righteous man, blameless among his contemporaries" who "walked with God," was a part of God's redemptive plan from the beginning (Genesis 6:9).

The entire world rejected God and told Him that they didn't believe or trust Him. But because of His relationship with Noah, God warned him about His coming act of judgment and told him to build an ark. And Noah obeyed. That act of obedience may seem like an obvious response when we know how the story ends. But Noah didn't have that luxury, and building the ark required an incredible amount of faith.

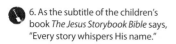 6. As the subtitle of the children's book *The Jesus Storybook Bible* says, "Every story whispers His name."

The world around him was rebelling against God. No one lived in fear of the Lord. Noah didn't have a community of fellow believers encouraging him to press on and keep building. The ark took decades to complete, and during that time everyone else was going about their normal lives, living however they wanted. Surely people asked questions of Noah when they saw the massive structure begin to take shape, and he must've had to provide many an explanation for the work to which he was committed.[7]

People must've thought Noah was nuts. I'm sure he and his family were the talk of the town, but not in a good way. Undoubtedly Noah had friends or family members who tried to reason with him and convince him that he was wasting his life. Can you imagine what Noah endured—emotional toil, social isolation, the internal voice in his mind wondering if everyone else was right, and wondering if he really was crazy? It must've been almost unbearable.

But Noah believed God. In his mind, the cost of *not* building the ark was much greater than the cost of building it. As far as Noah was concerned, the urgings from his friends to stop building the ark may as well have been invitations into his own grave. He trusted God, therefore he knew what was coming. Others would've dismissed God's warning, but Noah listened, and he risked everything to gain life and to honor God.

God warned Noah about the judgment He was going to bring to the world in the form of a catastrophic flood, but He also promised Noah that He would protect him:

> **"But I will establish My covenant with you, and you will enter the ark with your sons, your wife, and your sons' wives" (Genesis 6:18).**

God established His covenant with Noah, and his family benefited from the promise. Does that surprise you? Scripture doesn't name them as faithful to God, it says only Noah was. Yet, when the time came and their eyes were opened to the grave situation befalling the rest of the earth, they were counted among the saved:

> **"Then the LORD said to Noah, 'Enter the ark, you and all your household, for I have seen that you alone are righteous before Me in this generation'" (Genesis 7:1).**

God extended salvation and protection to Noah's family because of their relationship to Noah. He was the only person who God saw as righteous, but because his family "belonged" to him, they too were saved from the flood. Here we see a pattern for how God would eventually offer His ultimate salvation. In His graciousness, God granted physical protection to Noah's family because of their relationship to him. And in His

---

 7. Based on Genesis 6:15, "The ark was about 450 feet long (1.5 American football fields), 75 feet wide (7 standard parking spaces), and 45 feet high (a typical four-story building)."[ii]

graciousness, God grants spiritual protection to us because of our relationship to Jesus—His Son and our Savior.

Ultimately, Jesus is the One in whom God is truly and completely pleased. God affirmed this after Jesus' baptism, which inaugurated His ministry on earth:

> "And there came a voice from heaven: This is My beloved Son. I take delight in Him!" (Matthew 3:17).

As a result of the fall, no one is fully and inherently righteous. All have sinned and fallen short of the glory of God (Romans 3:23). No matter how much Noah loved God and desired to be righteous, he didn't have the power to save himself or anyone else from God's judgment. For that they were dependent on God's mercy. As Luke would later write:

> "There is salvation in no one else, for there is no other name under heaven given to people, and we must be saved by it" (Acts 4:12).

We're saved by the glorious truth that Jesus fulfilled every requirement of the law, and God shows mercy to those who belong to Him:

> "This was to fulfill the words He had said: 'I have not lost one of those You have given Me'" (John 18:9).

God used Noah to give us a taste of what was to come. But we must remember something important: Although God allowed Noah to physically protect seven members of his family from the flood, they were only saved temporarily. Ezekiel tells us that he wasn't ultimately able to save their souls (Ezekiel 14:12-23). Noah pointed to Christ, but He wasn't Christ. We needed a greater solution—we needed the Savior.

THE FLOOD

We also catch a glimpse of the coming gospel of Jesus Christ in the flood itself:

> "In the six hundredth year of Noah's life, in the second month, on the seventeenth day of the month, on that day all the sources of the watery depths burst open, the floodgates of the sky were opened . . . The flood continued for 40 days on the earth; the waters increased and lifted up the ark so that it rose above the earth. The waters surged and increased greatly on the earth, and the ark floated on the surface of the water. Then the waters surged even higher on the earth, and all the high mountains under the whole sky were covered. The mountains were covered as the

waters surged above them more than 20 feet. Every creature perished—those that crawl on the earth, birds, livestock, wildlife, and those that swarm on the earth, as well as all mankind. Everything with the breath of the spirit of life in its nostrils—everything on dry land died. He wiped out every living thing that was on the surface of the ground, from mankind to livestock, to creatures that crawl, to the birds of the sky, and they were wiped off the earth. Only Noah was left, and those that were with him in the ark" (Genesis 7:11,17-23).

These verses are challenging to read, but even more challenging is the thought that such a destructive event foreshadows the gospel. How could the death of a world of people point to Jesus' redemptive power? Where is the warm, fuzzy feeling I'm supposed to have when I think about God? Make no mistake, tragic though it was, the flood highlighted humanity's desperate need for a Savior and God's merciful plan to meet that need.

Some people read this story and conclude that the flood was simply God bringing an act of judgment down on the sins of the people. To them, the flood merely depicts an angry God giving humanity exactly what it deserved. Or worse, they see a helpless people being tortured by an awful God. But if that were the case, the story couldn't possibly point to the good news of the gospel. It would be a heaping dose of bad news, certainly not a precursor to good news.

We can't deny that God's judgment did play a part in the flood, but in the midst of His judgment, we find undeniably good news. In the flood account, we see God's merciful salvation on display in the lives of Noah and his family. When the flood of judgment did come, two things happened. On the one hand, billions of people drowned in the waters of their unbelief. They were swallowed up by the water in punishment for their sins. The flood was the greatest physical disaster the world had ever known, and it remains so even today. But on the other hand, the same waters that submerged a godless people lifted up Noah and the ark. Through the judgmental waters that crushed the world, eight people were saved (1 Peter 3:20).

The ark was the vessel God used to save Noah and his family from the flood. When we look at the ark, we see a picture of God's mercy and His desire to protect His children, even through the acts of judgment His just character requires. Likewise, God extends His mercy to us through the judgment that fell on Jesus when He went to the cross in our place. Because of the judgment Jesus received, we can inherit eternal life. There's no condemnation remaining for those found in Christ Jesus (Romans 8:1).

 Listen to "You Are Worthy of Your Glory" by Jon Shirley from the *Creation Unraveled* playlist, available at *threadsmedia.com/creationunraveled.*

THE RAINBOW

The waters subsided after 150 days, and God brought the ark safely to dry land. Noah, his family, and all the living creatures that were with them on the ark set foot on land for the first time since the flood came. Then God established a covenant with Noah, promising to never again send a flood that would wipe out all of humanity:

> **"And God said, 'This is the sign of the covenant I am making between Me and you and every living creature with you, a covenant for all future generations: I have placed My bow in the clouds, and it will be a sign of the covenant between Me and the earth. Whenever I form clouds over the earth and the bow appears in the clouds, I will remember My covenant between Me and you and all the living creatures: water will never again become a flood to destroy every creature. The bow will be in the clouds, and I will look at it and remember the everlasting covenant between God and all the living creatures on earth'"** (Genesis 9:12-16).

God told Noah that He hung up His bow in the sky. The bow God referred to is what we know as a rainbow, but the word used in Hebrew (*qeshet*) is also translated as a warrior's bow (as in "a bow and arrow"). In other words, God said He hung up His weapon as a reminder to His people. But what exactly was it a reminder of?

Here we see the first example of gospel foreshadowing in God's covenant with Noah. The rainbow was a sign of peace between God and His people. A time would come when God's rebellious people would once again be restored back into relationship with Him, and He would have no more need for a war bow. As we've already discussed, God must punish our sins in order for Him to remain just, so how can He promise a relationship where there's no more wrath toward those who sin against Him?

The famous preacher Charles Spurgeon made an interesting point in a sermon he preached about the rainbow:

> "The rainbow, yet again, is a token that vengeance itself has become *on our side*. You see, it is an unbroken 'bow.' He did not snap it across his knee. It is still a bow. Vengeance is there, justice is there; but which way is it pointed? It is turned upward; not to shoot arrows down on us, but for us, if we have faith enough to string it, and to make it our glorious bow—to draw it with all our might, to send our prayers, our praises, our desires, up to the bright throne of God. Mighty is that man, omnipotent is his faith, who has power to bend that bow and draw it, and shoot his prayers to heaven."[8]

---

8. Charles H. Spurgeon, "A Sermon Delivered on Sunday Morning, June 28, 1863, at the Metropolitan Tabernacle, Newington" [cited 23 February 2011]. Available from the Internet: *www.answersingenesis.org*.

Our sins were punished once and for all when God pointed the arrow of His wrath at His own Son as He hung on a cross. That was the final arrow of wrath God shot with His bow before hanging it up for good. Our God is willing to suffer so His children may live.

Another aspect of the rainbow that shows us the gospel is that you'll always find it where the sun and a storm come together. This tells us something about how God accomplishes His grace. As one biblical commentator noted, "The obvious glory of the rainbow, however, against the gloom of the cloud . . . arises from the conjunction of sun and storm, as of mercy and judgment."[9]

This is the contextual beauty of the rainbow. Its appearance at the conjunction of sun and storm symbolizes the meeting between God's mercy and judgment. Where is this divine place? The cross of Jesus Christ!

On the cross we see, yet again, the merging of sun and storm, the conjunction of mercy and judgment. This is the place where God poured out His infinite wrath against sin and His infinite love toward His children.

THE GRIEF OF CHRIST

We sinned against God, yet history continued on because God was willing to suffer. Think about it: You and I have life because God chose to suffer. Throughout Genesis and the rest of the Old Testament, we see hints of the sacrifice God would make for us, but it wasn't until God's justice and grace united at the cross in the death of Jesus our Savior that we were completely and permanently redeemed.

To what degree did God have to suffer that we may have life? Author and pastor C. J. Mahaney gave an excellent perspective on what happened at Calvary in his sermon, "The Cry from the Cross." Mahaney explained that the price Jesus paid was pain. His bodily pains were great—hands and feet nailed to the wood, and the iron breaking through the most tender nerves. His soul-pains were greater still. His heart was melted like wax, was very heavy, and was broken with reproach. He was deserted of God and left beneath the black thunderclouds of divine wrath. His soul was exceedingly sorrowful, even unto death. It was pain that bought us. But pain alone couldn't have redeemed us; it was by death that the Savior paid the ransom.

Yes, He experienced physical death as His lungs collapsed and asphyxiation led Him to breathe His last breath. But His physical death wasn't alone. It was attended by His spiritual death as He cried in unusual darkness, "My God, My God, why have You forsaken Me?" You see, this was the crucifixion within the crucifixion. It was the greatest protest ever screamed in human history—that a man who knew no sin would

9. Derek Kidner, *Genesis: An Introduction and Commentary,* 102.

become sin and be forsaken by God, and as R. C. Sproul put it, "This was the scream of the damned."[10]

This isn't the picture of the cross we like to consider, is it? More often than not, we thank God that the cross happened and are grateful for all it accomplished for us, but rarely do we dwell on the intricacies and the implications of the cost God had to pay for us to be reconciled to Him. I sure don't like to think about it. Our heavenly Father chose to demonstrate the fullness of His love by redeeming an undeserving people. And it cost Him everything.

I wonder what the world sounded like when God opened up the fountains of the deep and let the waters of His wrath fall on the earth. What a terrifying scene that must've been. I imagine chaos and horror. I picture some people trying with all their might to overcome the imminent flood, fighting with everything in them to save themselves, while others tragically accepted their end by letting the waters wash them away. The sounds surely amplified the terror all the more. Screams of people coming face to face with an end they never imagined and a judgment they assumed would never come. Screams of those who realized their futility too late.

The same scream sealed the grief of Christ on the cross. It was the epitome of His payment and suffering, the full extent of God's anguish to save us from His unbearable wrath. God aimed the arrows from His war bow squarely and intentionally on Himself, and He took them all. The judgment we deserve for each and every sin we have (and will) commit was taken out on Jesus, and in that moment we were covered in God's mercy.

The only right response to this truth is worship. This is the kind of truth that has the power to change you from the inside out. If you have the Spirit of God within you testifying to the beauty and glory of this gospel—a gospel highlighted all throughout Scripture—then your soul will sing of its greatness. By the tenderness of God, it will be stirred to suffer so that you may live; not just now, but forever.

The story we read in Genesis 6–9 of Noah and the flood reveals something glorious. Through this seemingly dark event we see a glimpse of preservation and hope. It's a taste of the greatest salvation in the history of the world.

10. C. J. Mahaney, "The Cry from the Cross," 16 June 2008 [cited 9 March 2011]. Available from the Internet: *www.sovereigngraceministries.org.*

Can you recall a time when you were truly grieved?

Describe how you think God felt when He looked down on our rebellious and sinful world.

Do you think God feels differently when He looks at our world today than when He looked at the world Noah lived in? Explain.

What are all the elements you see in the flood account that point us to the gospel? Are there others you see that weren't mentioned in this session? If yes, explain.

Leading a group? It's the way to go.
Find extra questions and teaching
tools in the leader kit, available on
threadsmedia.com/creationunraveled.

Based on what you read in this session, what are some of the similarities between Noah and Jesus?

What are some of the ways Jesus fulfilled what Noah lacked in redeeming others?

Compare and contrast the flood with eternal punishment and the ark with the ark of salvation.

How does it make you feel to know God hung up His bow of wrath forever? Do you live as if this is true?

What are a few things you learned through this study of the familiar Noah and the flood story that you hadn't thought about before?

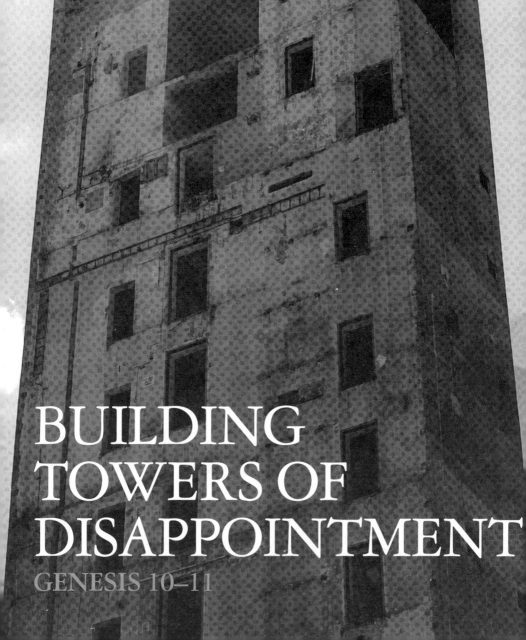

BUILDING TOWERS OF DISAPPOINTMENT
GENESIS 10–11

SESSION SIX

"At one time the whole earth had the same language and vocabulary. As people migrated from the east, they found a valley in the land of Shinar and settled there. They said to each other, 'Come, let us make oven-fired bricks.' They used brick for stone and asphalt for mortar. And they said, 'Come, let us build ourselves a city and a tower with its top in the sky. Let us make a name for ourselves; otherwise, we will be scattered over the face of the whole earth'" (Genesis 11:1-4).

The story of the Tower of Babel in Genesis 11 has transcended the Bible and seeped into our contemporary culture. The word babel still exists in modern English. It means noise or confusion, a definition that reflects what most of us think of when we hear the story. We picture the confusion that must have descended as people instantly found one another incoherent and their frustration as they sought to make themselves understood. The drama of this story makes it read like a fairy tale about people who lived in the land of "once upon a time." But the Bible isn't fiction, and we can learn a lot about ourselves from looking back on the lives of the people of Babel.

Genesis 11 describes a time when real people spent real days wandering the earth. Imagine waking up in the morning and spending your day on the move, traveling endlessly across the earth with no endpoint in sight and no answer to the common question, "Are we there yet?" "There" didn't exist, because God had commanded the people to "fill the earth" (Genesis 9:1). That's where Genesis 11 begins. Until one day, when something inside the people shifted and the desires within them drove them to stop moving and settle.

The heart of the story of Babel and its connection to our lives isn't in the city or tower they built, or in the confusion of their language. The heart of the story lies in the why. What moved in the hearts of the people to cause them to rebel against God's command and settle somewhere? When we examine the text, we see in these people evidence of three deep-rooted desires that prompted them to stop moving and build a city—their desire to belong, to feel significant and valued, and to be connected to greatness.

These same desires are at the root of every human heart. While the outward working of these desires may look different in various cultures and sound different in various languages, the root is the same, and Babel helps us understand that root and how the desires are manifested in our lives.

BELONGING—A PLACE TO CALL HOME
Identifying the Desire
After the flood, people began to settle on the earth once again and, as the population grew, people spread out across the land. Some of those people migrated to a land called Shinar and decided to settle there:

> "At one time the whole earth had the same language and vocabulary. As people migrated from the east, they found a valley in the land of Shinar and settled there. They said to each other, 'Come, let us make oven-fired bricks.' They used brick for stone and asphalt for mortar. And they said,

Listen to "I Surrender All" by the Justin Cofield Band from the *Creation Unraveled* playlist, available at *threadsmedia.com/creationunraveled*.

'Come, let us build ourselves a city and a tower with its top in the sky. Let us make a name for ourselves; otherwise, we will be scattered over the face of the whole earth'" (Genesis 11:1-4).

The first desire of their hearts was for *a place to belong*. Now, there's nothing wrong with a city. I (Matt) live in one. You probably live in one, too, or at least something similar to a city. Cities aren't bad things. A city provides a place to lay roots. When setting out to build a city, what the people really wanted to establish was a sense of belonging—a place to call home. A home was worthy of the bloodied hands, calloused fingers, and broken backs it took to build a tower of bricks. The fact that the people wanted to settle somewhere shouldn't surprise us. A home meant they wouldn't be "scattered abroad over the face of the whole earth," and that must've been a terrifying thought.

I (Matt) imagine you can relate to their experience. Many times throughout my life I've noticed a longing deep within me—a longing to belong somewhere. The feeling is usually subtle and difficult to put into words, but I know it's there. It's something akin to homesickness. I've noticed traces of this feeling for as long as I can remember. But the older I get, the more intense the longing becomes. Despite my own home and a family I love with all my heart, I never feel completely at home. I sense whispers of something even better.

Every once in awhile, I feel like I've pinpointed this phantom thought that runs through my mind. Not long ago, I went to Israel and visited the garden of Gethsemane. I saw with my own eyes the place where Jesus knelt and wept tears mixed with blood over the thought of being separated from God for my sin. Kneeling in the place where my Savior's tears likely fell brought a sense that I was closer to home in that moment than ever before. It was intoxicating. Sadly, it was also fleeting, a taste of something that wasn't supposed to be permanent yet.

Another time, I was sitting in a deer stand at dusk and God splashed the most beautiful sunset across the sky. The colors were like nothing I had seen before. I remember thinking, *This was made for me to see! Although I've never seen anything like this before, I feel strangely connected to it.* Then the sun set, and my longing for home grew even stronger.

At the time, I didn't know why I felt that way. But I do now. I never feel quite at home because I'm not supposed to. This world isn't my home; I'm just passing through. This place holds many blessings for me and a wonderful life, but nothing here will satisfy my longing for a home where I truly belong. That feeling won't be complete until I'm reunited with God in heaven and what was lost in the garden is restored again. No home or city I could build will make this better—only God will.

The Root of the Desire

The desire to belong resonates with all of us. It looks different in every individual, but it's cemented into the very foundation of our hearts. Think back to how it was in the beginning. In the garden of Eden, Adam and Eve found themselves in a condition that none of us can relate to; their deepest needs were satisfied. God gave them a home—a place they called their own. Being in the garden with God fulfilled their need to belong:

> "The LORD God planted a garden in Eden, in the east, and there He placed the man He had formed" (Genesis 2:8).

> "The LORD God took the man and placed him in the garden of Eden to work it and watch over it" (Genesis 2:15).

Moses emphasized the connection between Adam and this beautiful garden God created for him. We were created to belong in a place that was designed with us in mind. Think about that for a moment. Look at the broken world around you. What would it be like to open your eyes for the first time in a place that was designed with you in mind by the Creator of the universe? A place that you didn't just *call* "home," but a place that *was* your home, in the deepest and truest sense. A place that you were made for and that was made for you.

When Adam and Eve walked with God in the garden, do you think they had a deep, unmet need to belong to something? In a paradise that was designed with them in mind, do you think they felt like wanderers? In Eden, with the Father, they had a home that met every desire they could conjure. They weren't longing for a home in the garden. They were home.

But when sin entered the world, their hearts became consumed with the darkness that comes from exchanging the truth of God for a shallow imitation of His glory. When the garden was lost, the desires that were knitted into our souls didn't just go away. Our need to belong didn't disappear because we were cast out of Eden. On the contrary, when we were cast out of Eden we lost our home, and we've been fighting to recreate it ever since.

I imagine the people of Babel felt that need. Can you picture them tired of waking up every morning and feeling the ache for home as they packed up camp and continued their journey—tired of wondering what was next and where they were supposed to go? So they set their hands to build something that would finally make them feel like they belonged somewhere.

What Is Our Tower?

We do the same thing. Since the fall of mankind, we've been desperately seeking a home, trying to connect and find a sense of belonging. We turn to our friends, our jobs, and our possessions, thinking that if we can just have "fill-in-the-blank," then we'll feel less disconnected and more at home. For a lot of us, this involves filling our lives with meaningless stuff.

Materialism is one of the biggest idols in many modern cultures. We think that if we just get our hands on what our neighbor has, or what we saw on television, then we'll feel complete, at least for a moment. We try to plug that hole of emptiness with cars, toys, houses, and clothes. We make our homes here, forgetting that we're not meant to stay.

When we believe the lie that we can fill the chasms within us with physical things and neglect God, then waiting for comfort in heaven becomes irrelevant. Why do I need God when I have all this stuff? However, the "stuff" never fully satisfies our desire for our real home where we truly belong. One of the most gracious blessings God gives us is not letting that yearning for home leave us. If we get too comfortable in this world, we may forget that a better one awaits.

We were made for a place where we belong, and that place is in the presence of God. When we're with the Lord, we're home.

God's Solution

The good news is that God doesn't look at our desire to belong and tell us to get over it. He doesn't seem to think this longing is a sign of our immaturity and lack of faith. On the contrary, God seems to imply that the stronger our faith, the deeper our desire for our true home will be; the more mature we are in Christ, the more dissatisfied we'll be with this world. God doesn't ask us to deny our need for a home; He asks us to desire a better one:

> **"When the Messiah came, He proclaimed the good news of peace to you who were far away and peace to those who were near. For through Him we both have access by one Spirit to the Father. So then you are no longer foreigners and strangers, but fellow citizens with the saints, and members of God's household, built on the foundation of the apostles and prophets, with Christ Jesus Himself as the cornerstone" (Ephesians 2:17-20).**

In the story of Babel, it wasn't the people's desire to have a place to belong that was sin, or that their desire was too deep and vast and consuming. The problem was that their desire was too shallow and small, therefore they presumed that an earthly city could fill their need. Their sin was the presumption that they could make something to replace Eden.

 Watch the *Creation Unraveled* video
"Building Towers of Disappointment"
with your group or at *threadsmedia.
com/creationunraveled*.

We all have a deep and unquenchable desire to belong. You and I only have two options in front of us when we wake up in the morning, and they're the same two options that the people wandering through the earth faced all those years ago. We'll either spend our day clinging to the scraps of this world, settling for momentary satisfactions, or we'll turn to God to satisfy those longings and refuse to settle for an earthly home.

Open any history book, and you'll see evidence of the temporary nature of our earthly cities. Scripture doesn't mask their temporariness either:

> **"For we do not have an enduring city here; instead, we seek the one to come" (Hebrews 13:14).**

The mark of a Christian isn't that we suppress, ignore, or grow accustomed to our feelings of displacement, but that we turn our longings elsewhere and "seek the city that is to come." Our universal need to belong—to have a place to call home—points to another world. Because we were once at home with God, enjoying what He created for us, we'll never be content with this distorted version.

The Cost of His Solution

The danger of missing our opportunity to return home to God's presence one day is great, because to enter that heavenly city we have to renounce our earthly home. If we think God just wants us to desire that coming city *more* than our current city, we're mistaken. He wants us to want the future city *instead of* the current one.

We're guaranteed the promise of our eternal, better home when we follow Jesus. But to follow Jesus means abandoning this home, and that means trusting Jesus more than life. Unless we fully believe His promise to provide a home, we're unable to walk away from this world. How can we—who are made to have a home—renounce even a temporary one if we aren't absolutely certain a better one awaits?

> **"As they were traveling on the road someone said to Him, 'I will follow You wherever You go!' Jesus told him, 'Foxes have dens, and birds of the sky have nests, but the Son of Man has no place to lay His head.' Then He said to another, 'Follow Me.' 'Lord,' he said, 'first let me go bury my father.' But He told him, 'Let the dead bury their own dead, but you go and spread the news of the kingdom of God.' Another also said, 'I will follow You, Lord, but first let me go and say good-bye to those at my house.' But Jesus said to him, 'No one who puts his hand to the plow and looks back is fit for the kingdom of God'" (Luke 9:57-62).**

 "If we find ourselves with a desire that nothing in this world can satisfy, the most probable explanation is that we were made for another world." —C. S. Lewis[i]

This is Jesus' description of what it would look like if we turned to Him instead of the world to meet our desire to belong. This is His litmus test to see how committed we are to following Him and living with His kingdom in mind. Are we, like the people of Babel, settling for a home we built for ourselves, or are we willing to trust Him and long for the better home He promises?

Will you follow Jesus wherever He takes you? Will you follow Him to a third world country? Will you follow Him to a bad neighborhood? Or how about this one: Will you follow Him to your next door neighbor's house?

Following Jesus where He leads you is important, but of equal importance is following Jesus regardless of the influences of the people in your life. Will you make following Jesus more important than following your parents? Your spouse? Your children? Will you put the desires of God before the desires of your friends? Your employer? Yourself? Will you follow Jesus without clinging to family, respect, or approval? Will you look forward to that heavenly city without looking around to all that you long for here?

We all have things that define home for us, but Jesus said that it's ultimately supposed to be defined by Him. In Him we belong, and that frees us up to follow Him and have joy in all things:

> **"For we know that if our temporary, earthly dwelling is destroyed, we have a building from God, an eternal dwelling in the heavens, not made with hands" (2 Corinthians 5:1).**

SIGNIFICANCE—THE PROMISE OF WORTH AND VALUE
Identifying the Desire
The second universal desire that's evident in Genesis 11:1-4 is the desire *to have significance*. They built a city "for themselves" in order to "make a name for themselves." According to these verses, the people thought that a city with a massive tower would garner them admiration from others, which would make them feel significant and valued.

Not only do each of us long to feel significant, we have trouble believing we are until someone else affirms it. We need to have our value spoken into us. This was the desire that drove the people to build the city of Babel. They wanted to do something that would be worthy of someone saying, "Look how significant they are."

Another word that may help us understand what they sought is *identity*. We're driven by a need to secure an identity. We may first be identified as followers of Christ or children

---

 One of the most well-known towers in the world is the leaning Tower of Pisa in Pisa, Italy. When construction began on the tower in 1173, Pisans wanted "to show the world just how important the city was."[ii]

of God, but the world provides a litany of other identities for us as well. Identity is integral to the way we see ourselves and the world. Our lives must be defined—we must have significance—and a sense of identity is what provides that for us.

Every one of us has multiple identities. We're sons, daughters, mothers, fathers, husbands, wives, employees, supervisors, and so forth. We're also identified by character traits, such as responsible, trustworthy, intelligent, or funny. Each of these "identities" represents a different role we can occupy throughout our lives. These aspects of our identities are blessings, but finding our significance and worth in them is dangerous. If we're not careful, we can be more captivated by a function or role than we are by our identity as children of God.

In our hearts, we may know first and foremost that our significance is found in our identity as children of God, but do our lives give evidence of that? The truth is, we can be so desperate to have identities we're proud of or feel comfortable in that when we achieve them, we make them the defining qualities of our lives.

The Root of the Desire
Where does this desire come from? The people of Babel seemed to believe that their desire to be significant was in them because they were made to be creators. We still hear this today both in our hearts and in our culture. We believe the lie that if we can just create something beautiful or profound or necessary, if we can achieve something important, then we'll have value and significance. The people were right—we were made with the ability to be creators—but the problem was in their motivation for doing so. They wanted to create something in which their significance and self-fulfillment could be found. However, our motivation for creating things should be in bringing glory to the One who created us.

The root of our need for significance isn't in our capacity to achieve; it's in the reality that we were created. Our Creator walked with us in the garden and affirmed our worth by telling us how right, how beautiful, and how well we were made. Our significance was spoken into us by our Father. We didn't need to believe in ourselves because we believed God. We didn't need to approve of ourselves or one another. We had God's approval.

Do you think that while Adam and Eve were in the garden they longed for someone to know them intimately? Do you think they wondered if they were valued and approved when God bestowed on them His own image? Before that image was marred, they pristinely revealed the image of God in human form. Does that inspire doubts of worth? No, it couldn't have. With the image they were given, God deemed them the most significant of all His creation.

But when sin entered the world, it left a great divide between us and our Creator. We became deaf to His affirmation of us, so we sought that affirmation elsewhere. Our need to have significance didn't evaporate in that moment; instead, we became radically and recklessly insecure.

What Is Our Tower?

Building a tower may seem like a strange way to seek affirmation of significance, but we do stranger things in our culture. We're obsessed with getting people to tell us we mean something. The whisper of the news that we've made a mistake at work, or that someone is disappointed in us, can cause a tailspin of devastation. If a young woman finds her identity in her marriage and her husband is unfaithful to her, she may see herself as destroyed and valueless. For the man who sees his job as his foundational identity, losing that job feels a lot like losing everything. Because these identities are misplaced, they often cause us to live in fear of what will happen if we lose that role or function. We wonder, *Without this relationship or this job, who am I?*

When we think this way, we place our worth and value in the hands of things that are uncertain and unstable, and that's a dangerous situation to be in. We aren't promised that we'll always have our jobs. We don't have the assurance that we'll never lose our spouse or our children. By now, most of us know that we'll eventually fail in one way or another . . . or many. We can't live up to every expectation we have for ourselves, much less all the expectations others have for us.

So we build our towers of identity, just like the people of Babel. And when we do, we ignore the Bible's explanation that all those things we turn to for worth and value were never meant to satisfy the depth of our need for significance.

God's Solution

Our culture, and sometimes even the church, offer a couple of insufficient solutions to combat our desire for significance. The first option is to mask the need with self-esteem. Believe in yourself so much that you don't need anyone else to affirm your significance. The second option is to deny the need altogether. Many Christians mistakenly assume that sanctification is the process of decreasing your desire for approval. However, that's the opposite of how God intends for us to live. One of the marks of a Christian is the desire for significance—the desire to find your value in who God made you to be.

We're made with a desire to be told that we have significance, and we'll constantly seek to have that desire fulfilled. God's solution isn't for us to destroy our need for approval, but rather to increase and cultivate an appetite for approval that can't be even temporarily satisfied by anything less than God Himself.

God yearns for us to feel more significant and valued, not less. Why be satisfied by a spouse telling you that you're beautiful when the God of the universe tells you that you're "remarkably and wonderfully made" (Psalm 139:14)? How could a promotion at work add more to your significance than God's promise to entrust you with His gospel (1 Thessalonians 2:4)? Why seek the approval of other people when you have the approval of God?

Your identity was never meant to be found in the things of this world. You were meant to find the source and nourishment of your identity in your relationship with God, where it would be completely and eternally satisfied. He's the only One who won't and can't fail you. Your worth and value rest only on God's faithfulness, and He's eternally faithful.

The Cost of His Solution

Tragically, our desire for significance can become permanently distorted by the things of this world that we turn to for value. The longer we struggle to believe God's promise is real—that He'll freely offer us true and lasting approval—the harder it becomes to rest in that truth. Eventually, we become slaves to others as we desperately strive for their approval:

> **"For am I now trying to win the favor of people, or God? Or am I striving to please people? If I were still trying to please people, I would not be a slave of Christ" (Galatians 1:10).**

The people at Babel were trying to win the favor of others when they said, "Come, let us build ourselves a city and a tower with its top in the sky. Let us make a name for ourselves," (Genesis 11:4). Because they desired approval from men rather than seeking it from God, they had no hope of being satisfied in God or clearly hearing His voice.

To find your significance in God, you must refuse to seek the approval of others as a way of feeling valued. God doesn't withhold any good thing from you, and He spends His unending resources to fill the areas of your heart that are in want. He came, died, and overcame death so that you would have life today, and have it abundantly. Your search for significance is over.

CONNECTION TO GREATNESS

Identifying the Desire

The people we read about in Genesis 11 spent many days and years traveling throughout the land in obedience to the command God gave Noah and his family to repopulate the earth. After awhile, I imagine each day of traveling began to feel the same as the last.

 "Instead, just as we have been approved by God to be entrusted with the gospel, so we speak, not to please men, but rather God, who examines our hearts" (1 Thessalonians 2:4).

Evidently, they desired more from life, something greater, so they rebelled and settled in the land of Shinar, where they built a city and a tower.

Why would the people want or need a tower? Towers don't seem to serve much of a purpose; they're usually recognized more for what they represent than what they do. The most common function for a tower is a watch-post, but Genesis 11:1-4 has no mention of a need to keep watch or stand guard. A tower—especially an elaborate one—communicates something about the place where it's located. It suggests superiority and greatness and stands as something to be marveled at for its structural uniqueness. A great tower can cause people to want to be connected to it and the community it's in. It often makes them feel a part of something bigger than themselves.

The people in Babel saw their tower as both a way to attract attention and a way to reach into the heavens and be closer to the Almighty. For someone to possibly think that they could reach God by building a really tall tower sounds so foolish to us. But with the little scientific evidence they had at the time, they believed they could do just that. So they built their tower because they wanted to do something with their lives, and they wanted to be connected to something great. Theirs wasn't a shallow desire, but a desperately deep-rooted one.

The Root of the Desire

Like the other desires we've examined, the desire to be connected to greatness is knitted into the fabric of our being. God created us to be a part of something great. In the beginning, Adam and Eve lived continually in the presence of God and delighted in His perfection and His perfect creation. They were given responsibilities from the omnipotent God of the universe, and among those responsibilities was dominion over all the earth (Genesis 1:28-30).

Everything God made, He made for us to rule. He even gave Adam the power to name the animals (Genesis 2:19). Imagine encountering the first lion, eagle, or whale and having dominion over all those creatures. Imagine walking unprotected among them, fully aware that they would submit to you. More importantly, imagine what it must've felt like for the only uncreated One to entrust to you everything He made. Imagine the God of the universe delegating all His possessions to your authority.

While Adam and Eve walked in creation with God, the One who spoke everything into existence through the power of His Word, do you think they shrugged their shoulders and wished for something greater? Surely not! No one and nothing is greater. Before sin entered into the world, Adam and Eve met God face to face every day. Is it conceivable that in the deepest corners of their minds they secretly longed for a tower to transform the garden of Eden into something spectacular? No. I don't believe their minds could've dreamed up anything greater than the greatness of God they were connected to.

We long to be a part of something great because we were made to be a part of something great. We long to have power because we were given so much of it in the beginning. We long to brush against greatness because Greatness breathed life into us with His very hands and gave us His image to bear. The desire to be connected to greatness is a holy one.

What Is Our Tower?
We were created to live connected to the power and greatness of God. The people in Babel desperately laid brick by brick of their tower in an attempt to reclaim the glory they had in the beginning. The horror of Babel lies not in their desire to reach God's greatness; their sin was that they turned to brick, mortar, and the strength of men to satisfy a longing that could only be met in God. The offense of the tower stretching heavenward was the implication that they believed they had the power to reach God's glory.

Before you judge the people in this story for being so deluded as to think that a tower would actually make them great, reflect on our world. We try equally as hard to be connected to greatness, don't we? The desire can present itself in big, small, meaningful, and trivial ways. For example, have you ever noticed how we talk about our favorite sports teams? Perhaps the following statements sound familiar:

"Yeah, we won at home but then lost on the road. We just can't seem to win on the road."

"Can you believe that call? That referee is blind! There's no way we were offsides!"

"Did you hear the great news? We're going to the national championship!"

Really? Are *we* going to the national championship, or are the Texas Longhorns going to the national championship while *we* sit at home, glued to our televisions for four hours straight? We so long to have a connection with something great that we feel like we're a part of the team, even though we've never donned the uniform or snapped a play.

Obviously this is an example of how our desire to be connected to greatness manifests itself in a trivial way, but it happens in more dangerous ways too—ways that trickle much further into our everyday lives than sports. The need to be connected to something great can motivate almost everything we do, even the most important aspect of our lives. The root of this sin isn't found in our desire to be a part of something

 Listen to "Indescribable" by Laura Story from the *Creation Unraveled* playlist, available at *threadsmedia. com/creationunraveled.*

great, though. It's found in our attempts to turn to pathetic idols we think are "great," hold them up next to the living God, and proclaim that they'll satisfy us just as sweetly.

Our culture has a prescription to receive greatness: seek power, pursue renown. When we see something we think is greatness, or the opportunity to become great ourselves, we desperately grab for it, and often we get lost in its pursuit. We think, *I just need that autograph. I have to get another degree. If only I can get a few more Facebook friends or Twitter followers. Then I'll have something that will prove to everyone how great I am.* This desire is in us all. We've bought our culture's lie that greatness is found in earthly power and renown.

God's Solution
God doesn't ask us to abandon our desire to be connected to greatness. He asks us to abandon the hope of finding it through earthly means. Despite what many of us think, God doesn't think our desire for greatness is sinful. I felt so free when I learned that. I spent so many years trying to kill my desire to be a part of something great, but nothing I did worked. I would repress it for awhile, but it always came back in full force. I couldn't destroy the desire. When I finally heard that it wasn't possible for me to destroy it, I felt free. I couldn't get rid of the desire because I didn't create it, God did. And He created it for good.

God encourages us to pursue glory, He just prescribes a different means to that end than the world. God counsels us to humble ourselves and trust Him to bring us glory:

> **"Humble yourselves, therefore, under the mighty hand of God, so that He may exalt you at the proper time, casting all your care on Him, because He cares about you" (1 Peter 5:6-7).**

Our God delights in exalting humble people. He delights in bestowing greatness upon the seemingly unimportant. He calls us to reflect His glory by joining in His mission and defining ourselves as ambassadors of Christ. One of the best ways we can do this is by seeking to care for the lowly and the lost. He entrusts to us His ministry of reconciliation and invites us to care for the least of these in our society and pursue the lost. This means doing something that appears to the world to be the opposite of greatness.

The Cost of His Solution
Trusting in God's prescription for the pursuit of greatness takes a great deal of faith. He asks us to abandon our personal pursuit of glory and the things the world considers "great," which is impossible to do unless we truly trust Him to fill the void left in our souls. Many of us have a difficult time believing that obeying the call to follow Christ

and pursuing greatness in this world can't coexist. We believe that we can have both. We believe that God wants us to want Him *more* than we want power and greatness on earth.

We're not alone in that belief. Even the disciples—as they walked along the road just a few paces behind the Man who was the radiance of the glory of God—discussed among themselves who was greatest. Jesus responded by telling them (and us):

> "If anyone wants to be first, he must be last of all and servant of all" (Mark 9:35).

According to Jesus, the cost of finally getting our deep connection to greatness met comes at the price of renouncing our pursuit of greatness in this world. Without faith in Christ, this sacrifice is a gamble that even the bravest among us can't take. But God understands what He asks of us, so in order to build that faith for us, He threads promises of His greatness throughout His Word—promises like this one found in Psalm 91:

> "The one who lives under the protection of the Most High dwells in the shadow of the Almighty. I will say to the LORD, "My refuge and my fortress, my God, in whom I trust" (Psalm 91:1-2).

God also models for us in Christ what a life lived for God's glory is supposed to look like. Jesus knows what it's like to feel like you're fighting to reclaim a connection to greatness you once had. In the beginning, He was the One who brought everything we see into being. He had ultimate greatness. He was with God, and He was God (John 1:1-4). Yet, He left heaven and became like one of us. He must've felt that human longing to be a part of something great. Satan even sought to lure Christ from His ministry by reminding Him that He could have greatness and power in any moment (Matthew 4:1-11). Jesus was tempted to seek earthly renown.

But Jesus refused, and He humbled Himself to death on the cross:

> "Make your own attitude that of Christ Jesus, who, existing in the form of God, did not consider equality with God as something to be used for His own advantage. Instead He emptied Himself by assuming the form of a slave, taking on the likeness of men. And when He had come as a man in His external form, He humbled Himself by becoming obedient to the point of death—even to death on a cross" (Philippians 2:5-8).

The One who never had to endure separation from the greatness of God endured it on the cross. He felt the world count Him as insignificant. He watched the shadow of scorn cross the faces of the people He loved. He listened as His friends protested that He needed to make His life count. He listened as they scorned death as a waste.

And because of all this, God exalted Him to the highest places:

> "For this reason God highly exalted Him and gave Him the name that is above every name, so that at the name of Jesus every knee will bow—of those who are in heaven and on earth and under the earth—and every tongue should confess that Jesus Christ is Lord, to the glory of God the Father" (Philippians 2:9-11).

In Christ we have the ultimate model of humility and exaltation. Because Christ was willing to empty Himself and lower Himself, His Father gave Him a name that's greater than every name.

In our longing to be connected with greatness, we must trust the promises of God so fully that we relinquish all pursuit of earthly glory. It's not enough that we trust God's promises *more* than the world's, but again, we have to trust them *instead of* not only our world, but also ourselves. God invites us to join His mission and be a part of something great. Are you willing to be last? Are you willing to listen to the voices of friends, parents, family, and employers as they tell you that you're wasting your life; as they exhort you to pursue riches, power, and fame? Or will you trust that exaltation from God is best?

HEAVEN CAME DOWN

At the end of the story, God confused the language of the people and their tower became a monument to the differences we have. But this story doesn't only draw attention to the differences in our languages, it also highlights the similarities in our hearts.

When we think of our sin, we most frequently think about the visible symptoms. But is it possible that at the root of our sin is a deep desire that's impossible to shake because it's part of who we were created to be? Is it possible that our sin exists because, instead of trusting God to be both the source and fulfillment of our desires, we presume we know how best to fulfill them?

Is it possible that you envy your neighbor because you believe the lie that if you just had her car or his house you would feel like you belong in this world? Is it possible that when you lie to your boss, you do so because you can't bear to lose his respect and, with it, your sense of significance? Is it possible that behind your frustration with your children is resentment because you think they hold you back from being a part of something great?

Babel models for us the horror of idolatry and, ultimately, the terminal state of mankind unless we can be rescued from it.[1] The people longed for their real home. They longed for approval and significance. Ultimately though, they longed for all these things because they didn't feel connected to God. Their days of wandering, insecurity, isolation, and insignificance culminated into a plan; a plan to get back to "heaven."

The people of Babel recognized their separation from God, so they resolved to build a tower to reach Him. If we aren't careful, we do the same thing. Like the people of Babel, we attempt to build our way back to heaven. We recognize our desire for God, and we make a plan to get to Him. We go to church, we pray, we try to be "good people," we try to be like Jesus, all in an attempt to reach God by our own means.

However, no tower will reach heaven. If we trust in anything other than God to restore us to His side, we reject Him in the most offensive way. In the moments when we find assurance of our salvation in our own goodness, we hold up our hands next to the blood-stained hands of Christ and proclaim that ours are just as mighty to save.

The heartbreaking truth is that the people of Babel spent their blood, tears, and effort frantically trying to build a tower to God, when He was willing to come down to them. He saw us in our pathetic attempt to save ourselves, and He came down to us. Our God doesn't sit idly in heaven and watch us build futile towers. He left heaven and came down to get us. That's the unique glory of the gospel.

> **"For you were called to this, because Christ also suffered for you, leaving you an example, so that you should follow in His steps. He did not commit sin, and no deceit was found in His mouth; when He was reviled, He did not revile in return; when He was suffering, He did not threaten but entrusted Himself to the One who judges justly. He Himself bore our sins in His body on the tree, so that, having died to sins, we might live for righteousness; you have been healed by His wounds"** (1 Peter 2:21-24).

---

 1. *Idolatry* is best understood as people looking to something or someone other than God to meet their needs. That definition goes far beyond statues, golden calves, and primal societies, doesn't it?

In what areas of your life do you seek to have the desire to belong met apart from God?

Who are specific people you turn to, or what are specific things you do, to create a "home" for yourself?

How would your life be different if you really believed this world was not your home? How would trusting God for a better and lasting home affect the way you interact with:

• Your money

• Your family

• Your possessions

In what areas of your life do you seek to have your desire for significance met apart from God?

Who are the specific people you turn to or what are some specific things you do to make sure your significance is secure? Think of people, things, skills, or traits about yourself that, if you lost them, your sense of significance would be shaken. Also, think through what things make you happiest. What people or things add "value" to your life?

 Leading a group? It's the way to go.
Find extra questions and teaching
tools in the leader kit, available on
threadsmedia.com/creationunraveled.

How would your life be different if you trusted God to secure your significance? How would finding your significance in Christ alone affect the following areas:

• The way you receive feedback or react when challenged

• The way you treat people who are different from you

• The way you view the sin of others

• Areas of insecurity or arrogance

In what areas of your life do you seek to have the desire for greatness met apart from God? Do you look to your job, your ministry, or your skills and abilities to meet this desire?

How would you describe the mission of God? Does this mission seem great to you? In what ways are you neglecting His mission?

Do you see any symptoms in your life that indicate you might believe the aforementioned things jeopardize your acceptance by God? *(Symptoms might include: lingering guilt, lingering shame, arrogance when you succeed, fear of rejection from God, doing additional things to "work" your way back to God.)*

EACH DAY THIS WEEK, answer the following questions. Use the space on pages 128-129 to keep track of each day's reflection.

1. What specific sins did you struggle with today?
2. What could be the root desire behind each of those sins?
3. Find a Scripture verse that provides a promise for how God will meet that desire.

For example:
Sin: My boss told me we're meeting tomorrow and this has made me anxious because I'm worried I'm in trouble.
Root: I think I find my significance in what he thinks of me.
Verse: "The LORD is for me; I will not be afraid. What can man do to me?" (Psalm 118:6).

Spend some time praying for God to reveal your brokenness to you. Ask two close friends (who you trust and respect) if there's an area of sin they think you should be focusing on in this season. As feelings of defensiveness or frustration arise, seek to remember that your significance isn't threatened by your sinful state. Pray through the sin areas they mention, and ask God to deepen your view of sin so that you can trust more fully in Christ alone for your significance.

Look through your budget. Find one area where you can shift spending in order to invest in an eternal home rather than a temporary home.

Think of three types of people who our culture considers "less" or "outcasts." Where can you find these people in your city? This week, pursue serving them. Seek to do it in a way that brings you no glory.

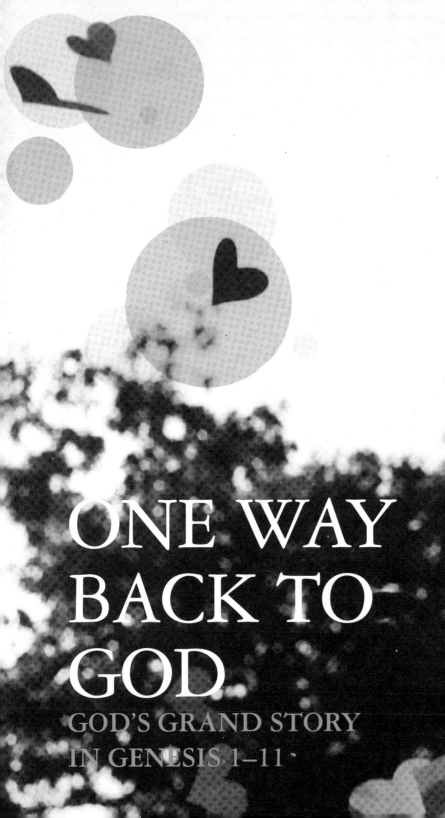

ONE WAY BACK TO GOD

GOD'S GRAND STORY IN GENESIS 1–11

SESSION SEVEN

"But God, who is rich in mercy, because of His great love that He had for us, made us alive with the Messiah even though we were dead in trespasses. You are saved by grace! Together with Christ Jesus He also raised us up and seated us in the heavens, so that in the coming ages He might display the immeasurable riches of His grace through His kindness to us in Christ Jesus" (Ephesians 2:4-7).

The first 11 chapters of Genesis cover some of the most profoundly gracious moments in human history. They include stories of great love and tender compassion between God and His creation. These stories give us confident assurance that peace between God and us will one day be restored. At the same time, these first chapters of Scripture give witness to some of the most tragic and terrifying displays of rebellion and judgment that leave us wondering if God will endure with such an undeserving people. Thankfully, in those episodes of darkness, we're reminded all the more that God's love for us doesn't run out, despite our faithlessness and rejection of Him. Though our hearts are prone to run far away, His love runs further still.

A RECAP OF GENESIS 1–11

In the garden we saw God prepare the world for the presence of humanity, His finest creation. We watched in awe as the same powerful, mighty God who spoke everything into being with the power of His words knelt down and gathered dirt with His own hands. From that dust He made man in His own image, a seal that was unique among all the rest of God's masterful creation. After shaping the first man's outer being with His hands, God breathed the breath of life into his nostrils. Such a majestic God also proves to be intimate and near with His children.

But then we watched in horror as our first parents, Adam and Eve, turned from the God of their making for fear that He wasn't all He claimed to be. They refused His love and set out on their own to discover everything they thought God was keeping from them. Sadly, they realized the error of their ways much too late. Their sin, which caused the fall of all mankind, placed a chasm between God and humanity that couldn't be remedied without divine intervention. Separation from God was the single most devastating event to happen in all of time, eclipsing every war, famine, genocide, and disaster.

Sin became the most alarming problem we faced. It infects every heart and leads every person into a lifetime of intolerable offenses against a holy God. The story of Cain and Abel showed us that sin was beginning to not only pass through generations, but it was multiplying as it did. Creation became so infiltrated with evil that God looked upon the earth and found only one person out of the entire global population who believed in Him. This man, Noah, and his family were preserved when God sent the waters of judgment to swallow the wickedness of flesh and cleanse the earth of its destruction. The remnant after the waters subsided would go on to repopulate the earth.

Unfortunately, sin was just as prevalent after the flood as it was before. In the story of the Tower of Babel, people came together to accomplish something great. But the

 Listen to "Hallelujah, What a Savior" by the Shelly Moore Band from the *Creation Unraveled* playlist, available at *threadsmedia.com/creationunraveled.*

greatness they sought wasn't God's greatness. It was their own. From the cries of their hearts for belonging, significance, and a connection to greatness, we see their longings for what was lost in the garden of Eden. In an attempt to deal with crippling loss, they turned to things of the world to fulfill the deficiencies of their hearts. As a result, they became idolaters.

Every story from Genesis 1–11 teaches us a variety of things about ourselves as people separated from God, our sin as the agent of that separation, and our God who's unwavering in His pursuit to win us back. Now that we've reviewed what we've covered in Genesis up to this point, let's do one last thing with these passages of Scripture. Let's look at them again. What? Why are we going back? Did we miss something the first time?

Well, yes and no. When you study the Old Testament, there are three different lenses you can use to examine the text: low-level narrative, mid-level narrative, and high-level narrative. In each session of this book, we've applied the low-level and mid-level narrative approaches to various passages, but now we're going to focus solely on the high-level narrative. Before we do so, though, here's what those terms mean:

The *low-level narrative* lens asks you to focus on the small and intricate details of the story you're examining. For example, if you were looking at the flood story through the low-level narrative lens, you would pay attention to details such as the animals coming in two-by-two and the size of the ark being 300 cubits long. These small pieces give the story its needed validity and context.

The *mid-level narrative* steps back from the story slightly to gain a larger picture. It scans back from the details and asks the question, "What is God trying to say through this story?" This is the way we often teach Sunday School and preach to congregations. If we were to look at the same story of the flood through the mid-level narrative lens, then we would observe the overview of the story. Humanity sinned. God became intolerant of the sin and decided to send a flood to wipe out most of humanity. God saved one family and then made a covenant with them that promised to never flood the earth again. God sent a rainbow, which reminds us that He loves us. This is the story from the perspective of the mid-level narrative.

Lastly, we have the *high-level narrative*. When using this tool to study, interpret, and apply Scripture, the reader steps back from the individual story being studied and considers it in light of the general counsel and story line of the entire Bible. This lens allows the person looking at the text to answer the question, "How do the low- and mid-level narrative portions of this story fit into the bigger picture of God's ultimate plan for redemption?" As we consider the meaning of the flood, we incorporate it into what God is doing in history and in Scripture.

With this perspective, we're reminded that the Bible isn't merely a collection of individual, unconnected stories. It's the compilation of hundreds of stories that all have the same gracious message woven into them.

One way to think about these perspectives working together to provide a clearer picture of Scripture is to envision a jigsaw puzzle. When you begin working through a puzzle, you may start matching individual pieces of the puzzle together based on the details on the piece itself. This is capturing the focus of the low-level narrative. Once you get sections of the puzzle completed, you understand more of what is going on within the picture. You don't have the full portrait, but you get a better idea of the overall purpose within the sections that have been worked out. This is what the mid-level narrative achieves when applied to Scripture. Finally, when the puzzle is completed, you're able to step back and see how each of your completed sections work together to reveal the entire picture. The same concept applies when you use the high-level narrative in studying Scripture.

AN EXAMINATION

Let's revisit two of the stories of Genesis 1–11 and view them through the high-level narrative lens. What do these stories teach us about God's definitive plan for redemption—His plan to bring you and me back into His family and to save us from the wrath He must pour out on our sin?

The Flood

Sin became a viral disease that grew increasingly worse with every generation that lived on the earth. People's hearts grew cold to God. They became apathetic and indifferent toward their Creator. They distanced themselves from God because of their sin, so God intervened. He dealt with their sin by sending a flood to destroy the evil that was ravaging the world. Everything was lost, except one family—the family of Noah.

After the flood waters subsided and the family emerged from the ark, it wasn't long before sin roared back onto the scene. As it turns out, the flood was only a temporary solution. God sent the waters from the deep to respond to the evil that was overtaking the world. Yet, when the results came back from this disastrous measure, sin survived. The flood didn't destroy sin.

The Tower of Babel

Next we come to the Tower of Babel. Genesis 11 shows us that sin was very much alive and the people were allowing idols to fill their hearts instead of affections for the living God.

They looked for a place to settle and a way to fill their desires for belonging, significance, and greatness.

They wanted the things of the world more than they wanted the Creator of the world. Idolatry had taken up residence in their hearts, and they had no concern or reverence for God. So, as He did in the flood, God stepped into their lives and dealt with their sin. His method of choice that time was to confuse their language and scatter them throughout the earth. But what happened after the dust settled?' Did that response rid the world of the sin that had plagued it since Genesis 3? Sadly, it didn't. Sin didn't die when the people were scattered and confused. Just like a weed that grows back time and again, sin continued to spring up in the human heart.

THE APPLICATION

Neither the flood nor God's destruction of the Tower of Babel solved our sin problem. Despite the extreme measures that were taken, sin continued its progressive destruction of the lives of the people of God. It seems that both catastrophic events merely slowed the progression of sin, which leads to an inevitable question: Why would God cause these events if they weren't going to fix the sin problem?

Until you look at the Scriptures through the high-level narrative lens, you may feel like God isn't all He claims to be based on stories like the flood and the Tower of Babel. How do these events reconcile with His goodness, grace, mercy, and unconditional love? How do you marry these seemingly unsuccessful attempts to address sin with the powerful and omnipotent picture of God painted in His Word?

Here are a few things we know to be true about God: He cannot fail. He's all-powerful. He's all-knowing. He's in control over everything. He's perfectly wise. Scripture confirms these assertions. He knew the outcome of the flood before He sent a drop of water. He knew it wouldn't end sin entirely. And the same is true for the Tower of Babel. As He scattered people throughout the earth, God knew it wouldn't permanently end the pains of sin. But the question remains: Why did He do these things?

A GREATER SOLUTION

The answer to this question lies in the high-level narrative of Scripture. The flood and the Tower of Babel were never meant to be ultimate solutions for sin. God knew they couldn't be, because they weren't sufficient responses to my problem and your problem. God didn't intend for them to be possible solutions; quite the opposite, in fact.

God showed us these things in Scripture so we would see that these measures couldn't solve our problem and to prove that even these extreme "solutions" weren't enough.

 Watch the *Creation Unraveled* video "One Way Back to God," available at *threadsmedia. com/creationunraveled.*

When you look at the high-level narrative, you see that these two events weren't failed attempts of God to deal with our sin. Instead, they were road signs that pointed us to our need for a greater solution.

To prepare us for His ultimate solution, God responded to the problem of sin with temporary solutions that highlighted the severity of our disobedience. A time would come when God would permanently deal with sin, and that act would pick up where all these other solutions left off. Without the various "pointer solutions" of the Old Testament, we wouldn't see the full beauty of the cross of Christ.

The flood account shows us that the death of millions upon millions of people couldn't take away the sins of the world. The death and resurrection of God Himself was needed. The Tower of Babel shows us that we can't climb up to the greatness of God, but the greatness of God must climb down to us. And He did so through Jesus, the ultimate solution to sin in the world.

MORE OLD TESTAMENT EXAMPLES

It's hard for us to wrap our minds around God's method of using broken systems to cause us to long for a perfect solution. Thankfully, there are many more examples for us to turn to in Scripture. The same thread is intertwined throughout various stories to allow us to see the greater picture of what God is doing on the macro level of redemptive history. Two other important examples of God's temporary solutions to the problem of sin include the Ten Commandments and the Old Testament sacrificial system.

The Ten Commandments

As God looked down and saw the extent to which humanity was sinning on the earth, do you think He believed the best way to get us to stop was by giving us a long list of rules? Had we shown ourselves to be great at being righteous and obedient up to that point? Surely not. With the exception of Jesus alone, no one in the history of all mankind has been able to obey God's laws. I know that I've failed countless times. How about you?

The First Commandment says we should have no other gods before God. How many times today has your heart's affection for other things (created things) exceeded your affection for God? For me, this can happen with things as temporal and passing as enchiladas. Sadly, though, I'm breaking the Commandment when my heart soars more passionately for Mexican food than for God.

Another of the Commandments is to not bear false witness. Do you struggle with that one? Sure, we may not be pathological liars who twist and turn anything we can into

---

 Exodus 20 records the Ten Commandments, but throughout the Books of Exodus, Leviticus, Numbers, and Deuteronomy the Israelites received additional laws God's people were to live by.

a lie. But do you exaggerate? Do you omit some details when you tell a story to make yourself look a little better? Do you tell those "little white lies" that seem so harmless? That's bearing false witness, and it breaks the command of God.

Lastly, let's consider the Commandment against committing adultery. You may not have cheated on your husband or wife—you may not even be married—but Jesus said that if you look at someone with lust in your heart then that's the same as committing adultery. Statistically speaking, most of us have done that in the last 24 hours.

In case you had any doubt, it's evident that we're not successful at keeping the Ten Commandments, and we're not alone. So, why do they exist? Why add insult to injury by giving us this list of impossible rules? Is God surprised that we can't keep His laws? Certainly not. God gave us the law to point us to our need for a greater solution to our sins.

In regards to the law, the apostle Paul said:

> "The law, then, was our guardian until Christ, so that we could be justified by faith" (Galatians 3:24).

We can't live out the rule book. In fact, we fail in our attempts. Even on our very best day of godliness, we're light years away from obedience. Paul said the law doesn't exist so we can work our way to heaven by obeying every letter of it, but so that our boastful mouths will be quieted. Upon its creation, the law should've made us take our trembling hands and lift them to our mouths in shock and horror of the task before us. We should've realized that we couldn't live in obedience to God's laws. But we didn't, did we? In our arrogance, we rolled up our sleeves and took a crack at it. And as you know, that didn't go well.

God gave us the law to show us the gravity of our sin and highlight our desperate need for a better solution if we have any hope of being saved from the wrath of God.

The Sacrificial System

One other example worth looking at that foreshadows Jesus' work of redemption is the Old Testament sacrificial system—the original method by which people atoned for their sins. Even though God's children were eager to prove to God their ability to keep His commands, God was fully aware that they were going to fail miserably. For this reason, He put a sacrificial system in place as a way for people to pay for the sins committed in disobeying the law.

God created a system in which animals like lambs, goats, and bulls were used as sacrifices for the sins people committed. In a symbolic act, the animals were killed and their blood was spilled on the altar within the tabernacle. And not only that, but God provided the people a day once a year, called the Day of Atonement, when the sins of the entire nation of God's people were declared to be removed by offering of a sacrifice to God.

But within moments, maybe even seconds, the people were sinning all over again. Almost immediately after they were made clean, they became dirty once more. This sinning would continue throughout the rest of the year until the time came for them to make another sacrifice, then the cycle would start all over again. They were clean, and then they were dirty. The sacrificial system didn't work. It didn't end their sin or cleanse them in a way that mattered.

In the Book of Hebrews, we read further confirmation that the Old Testament sacrificial system was flawed and incapable of removing sins:

> "Since the law has only a shadow of the good things to come, and not the actual form of those realities, it can never perfect the worshipers by the same sacrifices they continually offer year after year. Otherwise, wouldn't they have stopped being offered, since the worshipers, once purified, would no longer have any consciousness of sins? But in the sacrifices there is a reminder of sins every year. For it is impossible for the blood of bulls and goats to take away sins" (Hebrews 10:1-4).

The old system just didn't work. Plain and simple. So why did it exist? Why did God give a sinful people a law that was impossible to keep along with a system that failed to adequately cleanse them of their sins? Is it possible that God was, yet again, crying out to us, revealing even more clearly our desperate need for a better, greater solution? A better and greater sacrifice that would actually remove sin?

THE WHOLE PICTURE

These stories are not failed attempts of God to heal the sin of the world. When we study the stories of the flood, the Tower of Babel, the law, and the sacrificial system, we notice quickly that these are all dead-end streets that were used by God to make it overwhelmingly and abundantly clear that there's only *one* way to deal with our problem of sin. All of these stories are really chapters in *the* story God is writing to ultimately and finally deal with the sin of the world.

Written into every page of the Old Testament is a longing to return to God. And as we turn through chapter after chapter, we pour over the pages looking for the answer to how we can fulfill that longing. The flood didn't provide a solution. The tower couldn't get us home. The law only highlighted how far away from home we really are. The sacrificial

 Leviticus 16 describes how God set aside one day a year for the high priest to cleanse the sanctuary and atone for everyone's sins. This day was known as the Day of Atonement, or Yom Kippur.

system gave us a glimpse of what life would be like if we were pure, but it never provided us any real purity. Nothing worked. Everything was broken. God spends chapter after chapter—story after story—making it crystal clear that there aren't multiple ways to respond to sin and solve it forever. There aren't various ways for payment to be made fully on behalf of an enslaved people. There's only one way, and that's through the complete and permanent atoning of Jesus on the cross for all our sins.

Child of God, when you find yourself wondering (as we all often do) thoughts like, *What will You do, God, to heal this awful disease that plagues me? What will totally cleanse me from my filth and depravity? How can I escape sin's death grip on my soul? Is there a way out?*, hear the truth of God. There's a way.

Through the life, death, and resurrection of His own Son, Jesus Christ, God made a way for us to escape sin's grip on our lives. The only way we'll ever be fully restored in our relationship with God is through Jesus' sacrifice. He's the only sufficient way.

If you ever wonder if Jesus' work on your behalf is really the only way to be redeemed to God, know that you're not alone. In fact, you're in good company. In the garden of Gethsemane, while Jesus was on His knees sweating blood just before He was to go to the cross, He looked up to His Father and asked the same question through tears: "God, is there any other way?"

Jesus asked the very same question that we do. Even more comforting is that God answered Him in the same way He's been answering us throughout all of Scripture: *"Child, there's no other way. Every other way is insufficient. You're the only way to heal the sin of Our people and bring My children back to Me."*

THE ANSWER FOR EVERYTHING

Through Christ, God has made a way for our sins to be completely healed and for us to experience relief from their snares and punishment. Every story in the entire Bible is whispering that same theme—the favor of the Lord for a rebellious people.

Before, our sin separated us from God. A chasm stood between us and our Maker. No matter how hard we tried to keep God's rules or earn His favor, it was impossible to bridge this infinite gap. Sin was the cement that restricted our stay apart from God. We could do nothing to undo the damage we had done through opening our heart's door to sin.

If that had been the end, if there was no grander plan of God, if the mid-level narratives were all we had to bank on, then this reality is where we would've stayed. The state of our condition would've remained terminal until the dew of death was on our brow and we entered into our just and deserved sentence apart from God. The depravity we lived in while on earth would be extended into eternity:

> "And you were dead in your trespasses and sins in which you previously walked according to the ways of this world, according to the ruler who exercises authority over the lower heavens, the spirit now working in the disobedient. We too all previously lived among them in our fleshly desires, carrying out the inclinations of our flesh and thoughts, and we were by nature children under wrath as the others were also. *But God,* who is rich in mercy, because of His great love that He had for us, made us alive with the Messiah even though we were dead in trespasses. You are saved by grace! Together with Christ Jesus He also raised us up and seated us in the heavens, so that in the coming ages He might display the immeasurable riches of His grace through His kindness to us in Christ Jesus" (Ephesians 2:1-7, emphasis added).

But God.

Were there ever two sweeter words than this? The mercy and love of God for His children made a way to answer every demand of sin and justice in Christ Jesus. He's the answer for everything. He's the way that we're going to be reconciled to the God who's spent every ounce of His strength and passion to bring us back to Himself. Jesus is the way that we're going to have victory over sin, death, and hell.

Jesus is the answer for everything.

THE *HOW* OF THE GOSPEL

Now that we've been reminded of the great news of the gospel that's come to us through Jesus Christ, we can look to our present and future and worship God for the blessings we have through this exorbitant display of mercy and grace. We now have a hope that we didn't have before, and Jesus won't fail us.

Have you ever wondered how Jesus accomplished so much? Sure, we can accept the work of the cross because of the confirmation of the Spirit of God, who testifies to its truth. But have you ever asked yourself, *How did Jesus accomplish what none of the other events and systems could accomplish?*

A couple of things needed to be true in order for us to be removed from the plight of sin that has entangled us since the fall in the garden. First, we needed an appropriate sacrifice. We needed a Person who had never been condemned by sin to take our place. It does no good for us to have a guilty man stand in our place, because we needed someone who was innocent in every aspect of the law. Since we know that the Savior didn't come to abolish the law, but to fulfill it, then each detail of the law had to be kept perfectly:

> **"Don't assume that I came to destroy the Law or the Prophets. I did not come to destroy but to fulfill. For I assure you: Until heaven and earth pass away, not the smallest letter or one stroke of a letter will pass from the law until all things are accomplished" (Matthew 5:17-18).**

Not only that, but we also needed someone who wasn't born with a sin nature—the sin passed down through the seed of humanity. This is the reason why the virgin birth of Jesus wasn't just an impressive miracle, but an absolute necessity:

> **"Therefore, just as sin entered the world through one man, and death through sin, in this way death spread to all men, because all sinned. In fact, sin was in the world before the law, but sin is not charged to a person's account when there is no law. Nevertheless, death reigned from Adam to Moses, even over those who did not sin in the likeness of Adam's transgression. He is a prototype of the Coming One" (Romans 5:12-14).**

This really narrows the likely candidates for a substitute, doesn't it? Every person (except Jesus) was conceived through the seed of man. Let's pretend for a second that we could find one guy who actually fit that bill, though—just for the sake of argument. Would he be enough? Would his death on the cross be sufficient for all of God's children to be reconciled?

The answer is no. This perfect man would possibly be able to trade his one spotless life for the life of one sinner, but there's no way his sacrifice would be enough for all of mankind. We needed someone who's eternal—someone for whom the trade of life would be innumerable. The only person who fits that bill is God. One life of the Creator is worth all the lives He created. A man wasn't enough; we needed a God-Man for this to work according to His plan.

And that's exactly what happened. God looked at you and saw every single one of your sins. He saw every hateful action, every lustful thought, and every rebellious attitude. He saw what you did in the darkness of your own home, behind closed doors. He felt the rejection of your heart as it was more satisfied with the things He made than with Him. He saw the film reel of sin that plays within your mind throughout every moment of the day. He saw it all and was reminded all the more of the garden of Eden; these are all manifestations of what happened that fateful day.

God took every sin you have and will ever commit and took them away. He didn't take away some or most of them; He took every single iota of sin from your being and forgave *and* forgot about it. But God doesn't stop there, does He? He couldn't simply remove the sin and be a just God. He had to enact punishment, and someone had to pay for your sins. So God put them on Himself; He laid every sin that you have ever or will ever commit on His Son. Not only your sins, but every sin that would ever be committed by any of the children of God throughout the entire history of mankind:

> **"He made the One who did not know sin to be sin for us, so that we might become the righteousness of God in Him" (2 Corinthians 5:21).**

When you and I deserved to be destroyed, He destroyed His perfect Son instead. He truly takes away the sins of the world. He makes a way for us because He's the only One who can.

WHAT DO I DO FROM HERE?

As the solution for our sins, God the Father sent God the Son to live a righteous life that we could inherit and die a redemptive death on our behalf. Jesus' righteousness and redemption are gifts to us—we can't do anything to earn them. We aren't used to gifts as powerful as these, are we? Something inside of us wants to be worthy of this amazing display. It's like when someone invites you to his or her home and you have a dinner with that person. Before you leave, you feel obligated to invite him or her to dinner in return, right? Of course! We've been taught that it would be rude to not repay that gift.

But there's a problem with this line of thinking. Gifts aren't meant to be repaid, they're meant to be enjoyed. They're meant to be responded to and celebrated. We shouldn't spend the hours and days that come after receiving a gift trying to show we're worthy of it in the first place. Especially not with the gift of the gospel, because thinking that we could be worthy of such a gift only demonstrates that we don't fully understand the scope of its greatness. Maybe the most humbling and satisfying aspect of the gospel is the infinite depth of our unworthiness. This God who we worship has done this because of His worth and greatness—not because of ours.

Beg God to help you trust and believe Him in light of this great gospel. Ask Him to spend the rest of your days making your heart look more like His, and pray that you'd be given strength to endure when He answers that prayer. If you're like me and have been trying so hard to please God, take comfort in the reality that you can't please Him with your works. Apart from the blood of Jesus, you'll never be able to spin your wheels fast enough to undo the effects of sin on your heart. Rest in the completed work of Christ to heal your problem of sin. God has provided the greatest Solution to sin. It has nothing to do with you, but everything to do with Christ.

If you're afraid that God is going to give up on you at any moment because you just can't seem to get it together and live like you're called, repent and trust in the justice of God. He's already poured out the punishment for your sin on Jesus. Worship a God who won't demand payment from you for something that's already been paid by Jesus. Remember, there's no condemnation for those who are found in Christ.

You're completely healed and cleansed from all unrighteousness. Believe this message that's told in every story throughout the entire Bible, and you'll be saved. This is the good news. This is the gospel.

A PREVIEW OF *CREATION RESTORED*

The evidence of the gospel in Genesis doesn't stop with Genesis 11. It continues throughout the entire book. In Genesis 1–11, we've seen how God created everything good, and even though we broke it bad, He stepped into our brokenness and is making it good again. God is bringing redemption and restoration in the midst of our rebellion and ruin. But how? How can we once again be restored as His children? How will God be able to look upon us once again and see that we're good?

In Genesis 12–50, which we study in *Creation Restored,* the second of our two-part study of Genesis, God shows us how He's restoring the world back to Himself. He also shows us how we can enter into His redemption and restoration. He demonstrates this through three dominating figures: Abraham, Jacob, and Joseph. Through Abraham, God shows us that it's by *faith.* Abraham believed God, and it was credited to Him as righteousness. But after we've entered into redemption and restoration by faith, how can we be sure that we won't just sin again and enter back into the fall?

Through Jacob and Joseph, we hear God's answer. Two things threaten our eternal security in God. The first is our own evil. Jacob is one of most flawed figures in the Bible. His life was plagued by the evil and deceitfulness of his own heart, yet one statement of God keeps him safe and secure: Jacob have I loved.[1] Through Jacob, God shows us that our salvation isn't based upon our ability to be good, but upon His goodness of choosing to love us in the midst of our sin.

The other thing that threatens our salvation isn't just the evil within, but the evil surrounding us—the evil of the world. Joseph represents a man who's truly trying to live a life pleasing to God and yet over and over again he experiences suffering and evil by others determined to ruin him. No matter how much we try to live a life pleasing to God,

---

 1. *"As it is written: I have loved Jacob,*
but I have hated Esau" (Romans 9:13).

will the evil in this world eventually drag us down? Though it may seem like everyone is out to get Joseph, one statement of God keeps him safe and secure: What man meant for evil, God meant for good.[2] Through Joseph's life, God shows us that although it may seem as if things are out of His control, He's sovereign over and is orchestrating everything, including the evil and suffering in this world, for His glory and the good of His children.

So, this is what we have to look forward to in *Creation Restored*: We are saved by faith. Not first because we loved God, but because He loved us. And He is orchestrating everything, including suffering and evil, to restore us to Him. We hope you'll continue through Genesis with us.

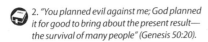

2. *"You planned evil against me; God planned it for good to bring about the present result— the survival of many people" (Genesis 50:20).*

Take some time to identify the low-level and mid-level narrative portions of another story from Genesis 1–11.

How do you reconcile the ineffectiveness of Old Testament events at solving the sin problem with the fact that God is good? How would you respond to the questions in the "application" section on page 135? Have you asked any of these questions before? If so, which ones?

Have you ever looked at the commands of God and felt like the Israelites? Explain.

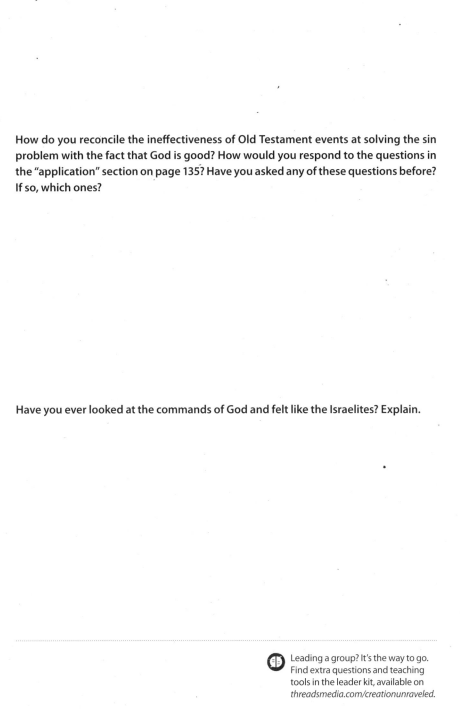

Leading a group? It's the way to go. Find extra questions and teaching tools in the leader kit, available on *threadsmedia.com/creationunraveled*.

Have you ever thought that if you just did a little better, then things might start going better for you? What was the outcome of trying harder?

How does the explanation of the purpose of the law redirect your thinking about God and the gospel?

Does learning about the weaknesses of the Old Testament sacrificial system convict you of ways you've tried to atone for your sins in lesser, inadequate ways? Why or why not?

Are you working to repay God for the errors and faults you've experienced throughout your time as a believer? What ways are you trusting in a system that won't work?

Through reflective writing or prayer, respond to the reality of the gospel in your life. Write down prayers of thanksgiving for Jesus' work to conquer sin, death, and eternal damnation.

How has your perspective of the accounts of Genesis changed as a result of this study?

How has your understanding of the gospel changed as a result of this study?

END NOTES

SESSION 1

i. If you're interested in learning more about the various views surrounding the creation account and how to reconcile those with the truths of Scripture, consider the following:*

Three Views of Creation and Evolution by J. P. Moreland and John Mark Reynolds

Darwin's Black Box: The Biochemical Challenge to Evolution by Michael J. Behe

Nature's Destiny: How the Laws of Biology Reveal Purpose in the Universe by Michael J. Denton

The Design Inference: Eliminating Chance through Small Probabilities by William A. Dembski

Science & Faith: Frieds or Foes? by C. John Collins

Signature in the Cell: DNA and the evidence for ID by Stephen C. Meyer

Redeeming Science: A God-Centered Approach by Vern S. Poythress

ii. Robert Jamieson, A commentary, critical and explanatory, on the Old and New Testaments (Genesis 1:1–2), (Oak Harbor, Washington: Logos Research Systems, Inc., 1997).

iii. Barna Group, "Most Americans Take Well-Known Bible Stories at Face Value," [online] 21 October 2007 [cited 10 March 2011]. Available from the Internet: *www.barna.org*

SESSION 3

i. Portions of Session 3, "The Goodness of Sin vs. the Goodness of God," were inspired by Tim Keller's sermon, "Paradise in Crisis," from the sermon series The Whole Story— Creation and Fall, preached on 11 January 2009 [cited 7 March 2011]. Available from the Internet: *redeemer.com.*

SESSION 4

i. John Steinbeck, Journal of a Novel (New York: Penguin Books, 1990), 108.

SESSION 5

i. Portions of Session 5, "The Sin of Man and the Tears of God," were inspired by Tim Keller's sermon, "Lord of the Storm," preached on 3 December 2000 [cited 7 March 2011]. Available from the Internet: *redeemer.com.*

ii. Dr. Thomas L. Constable, "Notes on Genesis" [cited 10 March 2011]. Available from the Internet: *net.bible.org*

SESSION 6

i. *http://www.goodreads.com/quotes/show/6439*

ii. *http://www.towerofpisa.info/Tower-of-Pisa-historical-facts.html*

Threads in no way recommends or endorses these book selections. They are recommendations from the authors and are provided as options for insight and contemplation.

Threads

An advocate of churches and people like you, Threads provides Bible studies and events designed to:

cultivate community We need people we can call when the tire's flat or when we get the promotion. And it's those people—the day-in-day-out people—who we want to walk through life with and learn about God from.

provide depth Kiddie pools are for kids. We're looking to dive in, head first, to all the hard-to-talk-about topics, tough questions, and thought-provoking Scriptures. We think this is a good thing, because we're in process. We're becoming. And who we're becoming isn't shallow.

lift up responsibility We are committed to being responsible—doing the right things like recycling and volunteering. And we're also trying to grow in our understanding of what it means to share the gospel, serve the poor, love our neighbors, tithe, and make wise choices about our time, money, and relationships.

encourage connection We're looking for connection with our church, our community, with somebody who's willing to walk along side us and give us a little advice here and there. We'd like opportunities to pour our lives out for others because we're willing to do that walk-along-side thing for someone else, too. We have a lot to learn from people older and younger than us. From the body of Christ.

We're glad you picked up this study. Please come by and visit us at *threadsmedia.com*.

ALSO FROM THREADS . . .

ABIDE
PRACTICING KINGDOM RHYTHMS IN A CONSUMER CULTURE
BY JARED C. WILSON

Because we're living in the middle of a consumer-driven culture, it's a constant struggle to fit the spiritual disciplines of God—such things as Bible study, fasting, and prayer—in between everything else grappling for our attention. Wilson examines key sections in the Sermon on the Mount and helps us come to see how these practices subvert the rhythms of culture so deeply ingrained in us.

Jared C. Wilson is the author of Your Jesus is Too Safe: Outgrowing a Drive-Thru, Feel-Good Savior *as well as articles and essays appearing in numerous publications. He is the pastor of Middletown Church in Middletown Springs, Vermont. Visit him online at gospeldrivenchurch.com.*

REPURPOSED
THE MEMOIRS OF NEHEMIAH
BY MIKE HURT

In his second Threads study, Mike Hurt examines the story of Nehemiah and helps readers realize how this great leader built much more than walls. In Repurposed, discover how Nehemiah reconstructed the faith of his people, and how those principles can change the faith climate of today.

Mike Hurt is the pastor of Parkway Church in Victoria, Texas. As a leading thinker and trainer for small group ministry, Mike is passionate about helping people connect in authentic relationships with God and each other.

SACRED ROADS
EXPLORING THE HISTORIC PATHS OF DISCIPLESHIP
BY HEATHER ZEMPEL

Throughout history, people have gravitated toward different methods of discipleship. Sacred Roads is an in-depth study of these pathways, examining the history of the church as it has followed Jesus relationally, experientially, intellectually, personally, and incarnationally. Discover the worthwhile attributes of each path and implement each expression into your modern pursuit of Christ.

Heather Zempel leads the discipleship efforts at National Community Church in Washington, D.C., where she provides leadership and vision for the small group ministry. She lives on Capitol Hill with her husband, Ryan, and blogs at heatherzempel.com.

FOR FULL DETAILS ON ALL OF THREADS' STUDIES, VISIT *THREADSMEDIA.COM.*

GROUP CONTACT INFORMATION

Name _____ Number _____

E-mail _____

Name _____ Number _____

E-mail _____

Name _____ Number _____

E-mail _____

Name _____ Number _____

E-mail _____

Name _____ Number _____

E-mail _____

Name _____ Number _____

E-mail _____

Name _____ Number _____

E-mail _____

Name _____ Number _____

E-mail _____

Name _____ Number _____

E-mail _____

Name _____ Number _____

E-mail _____

Name _____ Number _____

E-mail _____

GROUP CONTACT INFORMATION

Name _____ Number _____

E-mail _____

Name _____ Number _____

E-mail _____

Name _____ Number _____

E-mail _____

Name _____ Number _____

E-mail _____

Name _____ Number _____

E-mail _____

Name _____ Number _____

E-mail _____

Name _____ Number _____

E-mail _____

Name _____ Number _____

E-mail _____

Name _____ Number _____

E-mail _____

Name _____ Number _____

E-mail _____

Name _____ Number _____

E-mail _____